Why Can't I See the Angels?

Children's Questions to a Sufi Saint

M. R. Bawa Muhaiyaddeen

The Fellowship Press
Philadelphia, PA

Library of Congress Cataloging-in-Publication Data

Muhaiyaddeen, M. R. Bawa.
    Why can't I see the angels? : children's questions to a Sufi saint / by M. R. Bawa Muhaiyaddeen.
       p. cm.
    Includes index.
    Summary: A Sufi holy man answers children's questions and offers wisdom on such topics as creation, death, good and evil, faith, prayer, and the essence of God.
    ISBN 0-914390-62-7 -- ISBN 0-914390-63-5 (pbk.)
    1. Islam--Essence, genius, nature--Miscellanea--Juvenile literature. 2. Islam--Doctrines--Miscellanea--Juvenile literature. [1. Sufism. 2. Conduct of life.] I. Title.

BP163 .M769 2002
297.4--dc21

2002021096

Copyright ©2002
by The Bawa Muhaiyaddeen Fellowship
5820 Overbrook Avenue, Philadelphia, Pennsylvania 19131

All rights reserved. No portion of this book
may be reproduced in any manner without
written permission from the publisher.

Printed in the United States of America
by THE FELLOWSHIP PRESS
Bawa Muhaiyaddeen Fellowship
First Printing

Muhammad Raheem Bawa Muhaiyaddeen ☪

"My children, if there are any doubts in your mind, if there is anything that you do not understand, if there is anything pertaining to wisdom that you are unable to find an answer to, please open your heart and ask. It is your duty to ask your father. If your father knows the answer, he will tell you. If he does not know, he will ask and learn from you. Therefore, you must ask whatever is in your heart that needs to be answered and cleared."

Editor's Note

This is the third of many volumes of informal question and answer sessions with Muhammad Raheem Bawa Muhaiyaddeen (may God be pleased with him), a contemporary Sufi sage and mystic. This volume is specifically devoted to the many questions posed by children, ages three to eighteen. It is a valuable resource for parents struggling to answer their children's questions about life and death, heaven and hell, good and evil.

To make this wealth of information more accessible, the individual questions asked are listed at the beginning of each session, as well as in the table of contents. In the back of the book the questions are cross-referenced by topic, followed by an extensive subject index. In addition, there is a complete glossary explaining the foreign and esoteric terms that defy simple translation into English. Throughout the text you will find calligraphic circles (☻, ☻, and ☻) following the names of prophets, saints, and angels. These are traditional supplications and acknowledgements of respect, whose meanings can be found at the beginning of the glossary.

Bawa Muhaiyaddeen once said, "For every question, there is an answer." And indeed throughout this book and the volumes to come, he addresses our doubts, our confusions, and the heretofore unanswered questions of our hearts.

Introduction

M. R. Bawa Muhaiyaddeen often began his talks with, "My love you my children, my grandchildren, my brothers and sisters." We simply call him Bawa, meaning father in Tamil, his native language. Many of our parents came to Bawa at the ages we are now. Some of our earliest memories are of sitting in his room as he spoke and getting handfuls of candy from him afterward. While talks seemed to be directed at our elders, Bawa did not excuse us from learning by saying we were too young to understand. In this book are sessions in which Bawa invited us to ask whatever questions were inside us. His answers were those of a loving grandfather who gave the truth to us like candy, some to be eaten now and some to be saved for later. Not everyone lived near enough to ask outward questions, and others of us were too shy, but Bawa's words always reached us, soothing our hearts and easing our minds.

Children have an endless supply of questions. The world is new to them and each experience and feeling brings more questions than parents can know how to answer. We grow up thinking that despite everything we do not understand, our parents do. But we each have the shared experience of learning that this is not the case. Bawa's grandchildren were not spared from realizing that our elders do not know everything, but we were given one who accepted our questions with respect and offered deep, mystical replies—not just to a five or eight year old child, but to a fellow soul. As we learn about ourselves and God and find our way in the world, Bawa's teachings continue to guide us through life toward a growing understanding of what is needed for peace and what is merely excess baggage.

The depth of the talks in this book may surprise readers, considering the ages of those who asked about such topics as the creation of life, good and evil, religion, faith, prayer, and the presence of God in each heart. It may serve as a reminder that everyone has these questions within and having a teacher with true wisdom allows us to grow and continue asking, whether we are six or sixty years old. Though these sessions were between the young and Bawa, the answers are meant for all. They are as simple and complex as was right for the questioner and others present—children and adults alike.

Although Bawa passed away in 1986, his presence remains in his children's and grandchildren's lives. Growing up with Bawa's teachings of love and compassion among the difficulties of the world has been a different experience for all of his grandchildren, bringing us each to our own particular path of knowing ourselves and God. Whether we ask the questions outwardly or inwardly, whether we live a mile away from the Fellowship or across an ocean, Bawa teaches us that no question is ever too small or too large to be answered, and even if we do not understand it right away, its truth will be inside of us until our hearts are ready.

There are countless stories of how each person discovered Bawa, even from the children who always knew him. Often when someone reads his words or hears of the Fellowship for the first time, it is indescribably familiar to them. When asked whether he knows all of his children, Bawa replied that he even knows the ones who would come after his physical form passed away. Even though this book is of children asking Bawa questions in person, he considered all of us his children, his precious jeweled lights, even those who never sat before him.

Maryam Wilson, age 22

Contents

Editor's Note	*vii*
Introduction	*ix*

SESSION 1 (May 1, 1978)
Talk to a child mourning his pet squirrel.   3

SESSION 2 (March 2, 1981)
Advice to a young boy on how to conduct his life.   11

SESSION 3 (June 29, 1982)
Is there an animal heaven?   17

SESSION 4 (November 10, 1982)
A young child asks about where he came from and about death.   21

SESSION 5 (April 23, 1983)
What is the proper conduct between boys and girls
  ten years to eighteen years old?   31
I am ten years old and am wondering if it is proper to
  wear make-up.   32
What is wrong with dancing? Does that include ballet,
  tap, and dancing one does by oneself?   33
If we can't go dancing or play with boys, what can we do for fun?   36
How do we handle what our friends think about our Arabic
  names? People don't understand why we don't just go to a
  church or a synagogue like other people. How do we explain
  to them about the Fellowship?   37
If Adam and Eve ☮ had obeyed God, would the whole world
  still be a garden of Eden?   38

What does heaven look like?	39
If you go to hell, what feels the pain if you don't have your body?	39
Why did we choose to come here when we were already part of God to begin with?	40
Are there other people in outer space?	41
What should I tell my friends who told me God is just pretend? What should I tell them?	43
What does Bawa mean when he says God was never born and can never die? How did God come to exist then?	44
What type of Fellowship work can the children do to feel a part of it?	46

SESSION 6 (October 8, 1983)

How did Bawa get so wise?	53
If God has no beginning or end, how did He get here?	53
At what age do you think boys and girls should date, and at what age can boys and girls leave home?	55
Is rock and roll bad for you?	55
How does the heart move? And why can't you see the angels?	56
Why did God make satan if He wanted us to be good?	57
How can God be in everybody's heart if He is only one?	57
How do you know what people are thinking?	58
How can I go to Mecca?	59
Why has God chosen for satan to be evil?	60

SESSION 7 (November 13, 1983)

Can Bawa give me a special prayer to say?	65

SESSION 8 (April 18, 1984)

Why is the world always hard?	69
Why can't we see the angels on our shoulders?	69

SESSION 9 (November 10, 1984)

What should I say when somebody asks me what religion I am?	73

How does God take you to heaven or hell?	*74*
How did God make the first person alive?	*75*

SESSION 10 (November 17, 1984)

What happened to Adam ☮ when satan spat on him?	*79*
When babies die, do they go to heaven or hell?	*81*
How do you get to God?	*81*
If you see God, do you see Him with your own eyes?	*83*
How do you destroy satan?	*84*
How did God destroy satan? Can God destroy satan with His fire?	*84*
What happens to satan when he gets destroyed?	*84*
What happens when you die?	*85*
How do you get to hell or heaven?	*85*
Does satan take you to hell?	*86*

SESSION 11 (December 15, 1984)

Listen my grandchildren.	*91*
Is it good to give salāms *(greetings of peace) to people in passing?*	*95*
How did satan create demons?	*95*
How does God create angels?	*100*
If God is One, how could He be in everyone's heart?	*100*
How was God made?	*101*

SESSION 12 (January 5, 1985)

Why did God make the planets if no one lives on them?	*105*

SESSION 13 (March 15, 1985)

When you do the same bad thing again and ask for forgiveness, will God forgive you again?	*109*
When I hear bad words, I try to get them out of my mind, but they don't really go out sometimes, so what should I do?	*110*
We know that God will always exist forever, but will satan always exist forever?	*110*

When Bawa feels better can I sit on his lap?	111
Satan used to be good, so how could he be so bad now?	112
Why did God create satan?	113

SESSION 14 (March 7, 1986)
How do I find God?	117

SESSION 15 (May 4, 1986)
How come God made satan?	121
How come satan is bad?	122
Did God create heaven?	122
If satan was not here, would God be here?	124
Does God tell Bawa what to say, or does he just know?	124

SESSION 16 (May 8, 1986)
Why did Judas think that Jesus ☮ was bad?	129

SESSION 17 (May 25, 1986)
After a person dies and goes to hell, is it still possible for them to repent and go to heaven?	133

SESSION 18 (May 29, 1986)
How do you chase away fear?	137
How come God made people?	137
How do you chase away scary dreams?	138
How can we get our son up for early morning prayer?	139
How did God create the world?	140

SESSION 19 (June 2, 1986)
If there were no God, who would create us?	145

SESSION 20 (June 2, 1986)
How do you get over laziness?	149

What would it look like if God did not make anything?	*149*
Why did we come to this world, if the world of the soul was so good?	*151*

SESSION 21 (June 21, 1986)

Is there any benefit in studying Arabic?	*155*
If someone teases you for not eating meat, what should you do?	*157*
What prayer should I recite before a test?	*159*
How does day change into night?	*160*
Could Bawa comment on children who just sit during early morning prayer but don't recite anything.	*160*
Every time I want a toy, is that blocking my surrender to God?	*163*
How do I show my son that the treasures of God are more fulfilling than the things he wants in this world?	*164*

SESSION 22 (October 18, 1986)

In Maya Veeram, *why do you call it the ABCD world?*	*169*

Reflections	*171*
Glossary	*181*
Questions by Topic	*193*
Index	*203*

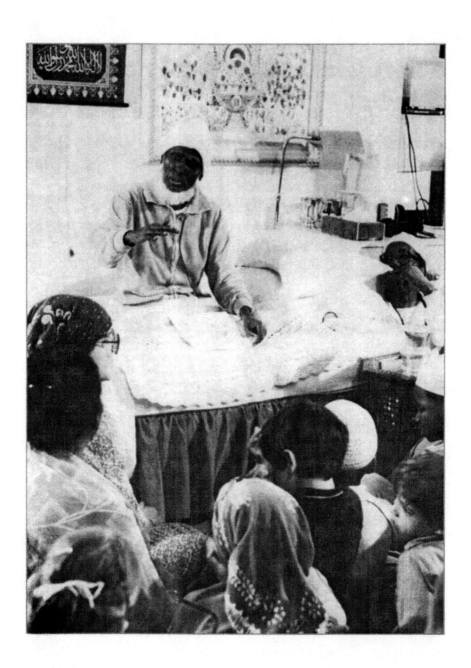

Session 1

Talk to a child mourning his pet squirrel.

Session 1

BRANAVAN GANESAN (age 10) (Branavan was raising an abandoned baby squirrel that he had found. One day, when he was carrying the squirrel on his shoulder, it fell off. He accidentally stepped on it, and it died. Branavan was very upset and came to see Bawa Muhaiyaddeen for comfort.)

BAWA MUHAIYADDEEN: Little brother, you are a good child, a very good child. Your heart is very good, and your compassion is very beautiful. The thought that you have in your heart is a very good thought. Your reasoning, your actions, and the love and compassion that you show toward other lives is also very good. Your love is like God's love.

I was the same way when I was young. I would cry whenever I saw someone suffering or in pain. If I saw somebody crying, I would cry too. That was my state until about eight years ago. Only then did it occur to me that if I cry when others cry, who will comfort them? After that, whenever I saw someone crying, I would smile and comfort them, even though inside I would be weeping.

In creation, there are five kinds of lives: earth lives, fire lives, water lives, air lives, and ether lives. These lives receive their nourishment from the five elements, and they would die without them. Similarly, man would die if there were no God. If God's food were denied to him, he would die. That is the difference between man and the five other kinds of lives.

If man would reflect and analyze with his wisdom, he would understand that each creation is bound by an agreement that determines how long it will live, and he would know how much time is allotted to each creation before it changes over and is destroyed. Man is the only one who can understand all this. Because he possesses divine wisdom *(gnānam)* and a soul, which is the power of wisdom, and because he also has the judgment capable of controlling and assessing everything, this gives him the capacity to understand the right and wrong in what happens.

From the tiniest atom, to the earth with its precious stones, to the grass, weeds, trees, shrubs, creepers, insects, worms, and the various types of foods and fruits—all creations need the five elements in order to stay alive. They need water, air, earth, ether, the warmth of fire, the different colors, and illusion and its glitters. And every life is governed by an agreement concerning its limit, but only man has the capacity to understand those agreements.

Now suppose you sow some seeds. When a seedling grows, you feel joyful. You are able to protect it and help it grow, and later its crop can benefit mankind. But since weeds grow faster than plants, they might strangle some of them, or worms might eat them, or winds and heavy rains might destroy them. They could even die from the intense heat of the sun or because they don't get enough water. Should you feel sad about this? No, you carried out your duty correctly and did what you had to do. But you need to realize that the very thing that helps something to grow can also cause its destruction. You should not feel sad about that. Your duty is to pour the water, spread the fertilizer, pull out the weeds, and protect the crop. That is your duty. Other than that, should you feel sorry about things that occur above and beyond your duty? No, you shouldn't. When such things happen, you must say, "This is not the result of my actions. Everything happens in keeping with God's will. Nothing happens because of my deeds. I performed my duty correctly and did nothing wrong. What happens beyond that is God's duty. It is the duty of the One who created." You must reflect on this with your wisdom. Do you understand? You must realize, "It's all right, that life's agreement was over." You need not feel sorrow.

Suppose the allotted time for a particular crop to grow and ripen is between three and four months. What is your duty? You must harvest it at the proper time. If you don't, it will perish anyway, on its own, because that is all the time it has to live, according to its agreement. If you do not make use of it at the right time, it will just decay. Should you feel sorry about that? No, that is its agreement. Even though you protected the crop and helped it to grow, it is impossible to keep it past that time. For example, when we harvest rice, before we can store the grains, we must separate them from the husks. Even then, we can only keep the rice for a little while longer, or it will become infested with insects and be devoured. Why should we feel sorry about that? That is nature. These things happen naturally.

Suppose you grow a nice apple tree, giving it water and fertilizer, and then it produces beautiful fruits. After the apples ripen, they have to fall from the tree. That is their agreement, or limit. Should you feel sad about that? No. Your duty is to carefully pluck them before they fall and then either eat them or sell them. If we use our wisdom, we will know what we should do. You must not feel sad about their end. Or, say some nice grass is growing in your yard. If you tie a cow there, it will eat all the grass. Should you feel sorry when the grass is gone? No, you should not think like that.

Man has to think about these things with his wisdom. All lives are limited by some agreement. There are earth lives, water lives, fire lives, air lives, and ether lives. These lives do not have divine analytic wisdom. They have only three levels of consciousness—feeling, awareness, and intellect. If they have an itch, they will scratch. If they are hit, they will run. They defecate where they eat, and sleep where they defecate. This is how cows, goats, reptiles, and other lives behave. Do they have divine analytic wisdom? No. Do they know what is clean or unclean, or good or bad? No. It is natural that we raise these lives, and it is also natural that they will do what they do. But sometimes their actions subject them to certain accidents. In this world, lives catch and eat other lives. So, there is always the possibility of accidents happening.

Say you are lovingly raising a goat, but it wanders off and is caught by a wolf or a tiger. Should you grieve and cry about that? Or suppose the goat goes out to graze and falls off a mountain. Because it has no wisdom, it fell and met with a sad death. Should you grieve or cry because of that? No. One who has divine analytic wisdom must protect a life that does not have that wisdom or use it, but beyond that he is not responsible.

Now, let us consider your squirrel. You intended to look after the squirrel. That was certainly your duty. If it had been left outside, a crow might have carried it away. Even if a crow didn't carry it away, a cat might have caught it. Or if a cat didn't catch it, a dog might have caught it. If a dog didn't catch it, a hawk might have swooped down on it, or a snake might have swallowed it. You saved that squirrel from all those possible accidents. It is all right for you to protect an animal that does not have divine analytic wisdom, but you might have kept it in a cage. However, because of your love for it, you carried it around on your shoulder. Since the squirrel has no wisdom, it fell off, and you stepped on it. Was that your fault? No. All along that squirrel was meant to die, one way or another. Sometime or other it had to go. In any case, it had to die within three years. That is the extent of its life. So why do you feel sad? Did you make this happen? No. You did your duty. What happens beyond that is not your duty.

Did you do it knowingly? No. You did not know that was going to happen. If you had done it deliberately, then you could cry, because a little bit of sin would have been attached to that deed, and the responsibility would have remained with you. That would be the opposite of compassion. But you did not know this would happen. You could have used your wisdom and thought, "This animal has no analytic wisdom. I should keep it in a place it should be kept. Even though I have love for it, I should not carry it on my shoulder. It might have an accident. If it jumps one way, a dog or a cat might catch it. If it jumps the other way and climbs up on something, a crow might catch it. Because it could be subject to so many accidents, I should keep it in a cage." This is what you might have done. But even so, why should you feel sad? All of God's creations are like this.

If you feel so sad about this, how can you bear to live in this body? We, too, have a body, and one day or another we will have to leave our body behind and go. Like this, every life has to give up its body sometime and return to its source. Earth lives will return to the earth, fire lives to fire, water lives to water, air lives to air, and illusory lives will join with illusion. Each one will go back to its own life force *(sakthi)*. But a human being has to join God. Why? Human life is God's treasure, and it must go back to Him.

In the future, do not let your mind dwell on these things. If you look around, you will see that all lives are limited by an agreement. To the extent that it is possible, we must protect what we can. But beyond that, we have to say, "There is nothing I can do. My actions cannot accomplish anything else. O God, everything happens as a result of Your doing," and we must hand over all responsibility to Him. Do you understand?

That is how you must act. Don't cry. You are crying, your father is crying, your mother is crying, and your sisters are crying. It shouldn't be like this. Make your heart strong. Use your wisdom. You certainly should have compassion for all lives, but then you must reflect on that duty and hand over the responsibility to God. Do you understand what I have said?

Now you have a parrot, and you are raising it with a lot of love. Let's say that one day you forget to close the door, and the parrot escapes and is caught by a cat. Should you grieve about that? Or let's say the parrot flies away and is caught by a hawk. Should you feel sad about that?

Instead of worrying about that parrot, realize that we all are raising a parrot within the cage of our body. That parrot is our mind, and it is always chattering and squawking and flying here and there. First we have to discover how to raise the parrot that is within us. We must learn how to control it and train it with our wisdom. If we let this mind constantly squawk and fly about, what will our life be like? What will our future be? We will die, having wasted our life. The world will laugh at us, because, although we were born as such rare beings, we will have wasted our life. After all our searching, we will have gone to our death in this state.

This mind is a parrot that simply repeats whatever it hears people say. If someone laughs, it laughs. If someone whistles, it whistles. Such is our mind. Whatever it reads in a book, it repeats over and over again. If we could make that parrot stop its squawking, it would be very good. But if we allow our mind to make all these noises, we will definitely have a lot of trouble in our life. We must correct and train the parrot within us and give it peace. That will be good. Do you understand?

That is what you must try to do in the future, little brother. Do not let your mind suffer so much. Do not let your heart tremble over something like this. This is a very small matter. It is God's responsibility. It is not your fault. Your duty goes only so far and no further. Use your wisdom in everything. You must not cry. Do you understand? You need to reflect on this. Wipe your tears. If this had not happened, the squirrel would have been caught by a crow or a cat or something else. It was not your fault at all. What happened was according to its agreement. You need not feel sad about that.

Look with wisdom. If you had analyzed with wisdom, this sorrow would not have come to you. All right? Now smile!

May 1, 1978

Session 2

Advice to a young boy on how to conduct his life.
11

Session 2

BAWA MUHAIYADDEEN: Raheem, in bygone days, sailors would place their faith in Allah, hoist the sail up the mast, and set out to fish in the big ocean. There they might encounter mighty waves, gales, and storms. Whales and huge fish such as sharks and swordfish would sometimes attack them.

Similarly, Raheem, our boat of life travels in the ocean of illusion. Many dangers come to us during this journey of life. And because of those dangers, we must place our trust in Allah while sailing this boat.

The first word you must say is, *"Bismillāhir-Rahmānir-Rahīm:* In the name of God, the Most Merciful, Most Compassionate." Whatever journey you undertake in this life, when you leave your house, first place your right foot forward, trusting in Allah. Let Prophet Muhammad, the *Rasūl* (the Messenger) , go in front of you and lead the way. Say, *"Yā Allāh,* I am starting my journey believing in You. Protect me so that no difficulties or dangers arise during this journey. Protect me so that my life does not capsize in this ocean of illusion. Until I reach You and join You, please see that nothing comes to overturn me. Grant me Your grace so I will conduct my life on the straight path. Be my guide on this path, so that I may live within You and Your grace and good qualities and actions, so that I may imbibe Your good conduct and act accordingly, and so that I may walk on the straight path to reach You. Show me that path and grant me Your grace. *Āmīn."* You must say this, and put your right foot forward first.

Raheem, in the morning, as soon as you get up, you must establish this intention. Later, when you step out of the house, put your right foot first, saying, *"Bismillāhir-Rahmānir-Rahīm.* Allah, I am in Your trust." Right foot first, then left, then right, then left. Next say, *"Lā ilāha:* There is nothing other than You," every time you put your left foot forward and *"illallāh:* Only You are God," when you put your right foot forward. Walk in this manner while saying that. This will be your life's journey. Wherever you go, say it like this. In the journey of your life on this ocean of illusion, keep this remembrance of God. As you place one foot after the other, with each breath, say this *dhikr* with the intention, "You must show me the straight way on Your path," and walk on. This is how you need to travel on your life's journey.

You must never tell lies. You must not waste your time or play useless games. Your journey must be conducted with Allah's qualities and conduct. You must not hit other children or hurt any life. You must consider all lives as your own and look at their suffering as your own and then help them. Whenever others are ill, you must say, "Allah, O *Rahmān*, O Merciful One, help them," and then you must offer whatever help you can. If others are hungry, you must share with them whatever food or water you have. You must dispel the fire of their hunger and help them quench their thirst. You must carry them and protect them. You must not talk about other people behind their backs. You must not backbite or tell lies about other people. You must not copy the faults of others.

Allah, the One, does exist. He knows every breath taken and every word spoken, and He is the One who passes judgment on all actions, not us. We must not try to do His work. Judging others is not our work, it is the work of Allah, the Creator. Accepting prayers is His work. Giving sustenance is His work. Giving life and protecting us—that is His work. Therefore, we must acquire His qualities, give all responsibility to Him, and remain under His protection. We must be in this state to do our work. Going on the straight path, Raheem, is the exalted state for our lives.

You must not smoke marijuana. You must not drink alcohol or take any drugs. You must not kill any animal or fish and then eat its flesh. Its life is just like your own. If we would cut our own flesh and eat it, imagine how much it would hurt. Or if someone would cut our flesh and give it to another, imagine how much suffering we would feel. In the same way, we must not intend to hurt or eat the flesh of other lives. It is wrong to kill another life and eat its flesh in order to make our own body grow. With Allah's compassionate qualities, we must eat the food of Allah's grace. Raheem, do you understand?

God gave you sweet candy. Take whatever He gives you. If you receive a lot, that is good, but if you only get a little, that is good, too. Say, *"Bismillāhir-Rahmānir-Rahīm,"* and eat. If you receive a large amount, praise Allah, and if you get less, say, *"Al-hamdu lillāh:* All praise is to God, I am content."

In this way, whether we receive a lot or a little in life, we must be content, saying, "Whatever Allah gives is enough for me." With faith, certitude, and love, we must make our hearts full. That fullness will bring us patience, contentment, trust in God, and praise of God *(sabūr, shakūr, tawakkul,* and *al-hamdu lillāh).* This is what we must have.

You must never be angry with anyone. Anger is a sin. The fire of anger leads you to hell. It is the *guru* of sin. Arrogance, hastiness, anger, 'I', 'mine', pride, jealousy, treachery, deceit, backbiting, and the separations caused by 'I am different, you are different'—all these will take you to hell. You must never have any of these qualities in your heart or in your body. Allah's patience, His contentment, trust in Him, and praise of Him are what you must keep in your heart.

In this way, conduct your life with patience saying, *"Bismillāhir-Rahmānir-Rahīm."* Put your right foot forward first, and say, "All praise is to God. All trust is in God. *Bismillāhir-Rahmānir-Rahīm. Yā Rasūlullāh,* go before me as my guide in this life of illusion. Lead me and protect me."

Raheem, this is how you must conduct your life. Raheem, do you understand? Do you understand?

RAHEEM CONNELLY (age 4): Yes.

BAWA MUHAIYADDEEN: *Āmīn.* You are a good boy, a good son. My love you.

March 2, 1981

Session 3

Is there an animal heaven?

Session 3

SALIHU AIGNER (age 11): Is there an animal heaven?

BAWA MUHAIYADDEEN: There may be. God created earth for the grass, weeds, and trees. And for the animals He made caves in the mountains and dens among the trees. For every one of His creations He has provided a dwelling in different places. He has given food and a home for everything.

There is a kingdom of God and a kingdom of hell. There are six kinds of lives: earth life, fire life, air life, water life, ether life, and human life, which is the light life, God's light life. There is a place for all six kinds of lives, but what is called heaven is for mankind only, for human lives. Earth lives go back to the earth. Some lives have places in the ether and some in the earth. Other lives, such as animals, exist as forms and as subtle forms. The only life that exists as light is the human life.

So, for the first five kinds of lives, God has kept five places, and each will return to its own place. If an animal does its work properly, it will receive its rightful place, but if it harms anyone, then it will be given the house known as hell, which God created for it. For lives such as worms, weeds, snakes, and scorpions, there is a hell, but any life that does good will be given the place set aside for its particular life-form (that of earth, fire, water, air, or ether). Only if it causes harm will it be given the worst part of hell, the worm-infested hell.

Human beings, who have the life of the resplendent soul, are the only lives endowed with divine analytic wisdom. Only those with this wisdom are entitled to go to heaven and can know the secret of heaven. Each other form of life has its own place. Animals eat and sleep where they defecate. But when you go to the bathroom, you wash and clean yourself. Animals don't do that. They do not have divine analytic wisdom. You may raise a horse or a cow in a good way, but it will still urinate and defecate and then lie down to sleep in the same dirty spot. When animals get up, do they wash their hands and feet? No. Do they clean themselves? No. Therefore, they will be given a place appropriate to their actions. Why? Because they do not have the awareness of divine analytic wisdom that shows them the difference between cleanliness and filth. They do not have that understanding, so they are unable to do the work man can do. They do not know the difference between right and wrong, or pure and impure.

A life that does not know the difference between right and wrong resides in hell without realizing it. It is only after one understands the difference between right and wrong and clean and unclean that he can realize the difference between heaven and hell. If an animal sees no difference between pure and impure, if it eats in a place of hell, sleeps in a place of hell, and lives in a place of hell, then that is the place it will receive in the hereafter. And that will be a place of happiness for that animal. Once it reaches a state of understanding, even if it is a cow, it will receive a good place. But as long as it does not have that understanding, it will receive a place befitting its level. This is how it is for the five lives.

However, if you can raise an animal in a good way, and if human wisdom dawns in that animal and you can train it to understand the difference between right and wrong, that animal will receive the heaven set aside for animals, the heaven appropriate for its life-form. Just as God has given animals a place here, He has also kept a place for them there. It is not really heaven; it is a place where they can live in peace afterwards. He has kept a place for each of the six kinds of lives to live in peace. That is His secret. For mankind, there is definitely a heaven. What others attain will depend upon their search.

June 29, 1982

Session 4

A young child asks about where he came from
and about death.

Session 4

BAWA MUHAIYADDEEN: Children, tell us your questions. Is there something you would like to know? My love you, my grandson. Let us hear your questions. What did you ask your mother?

GAIL NIGRO MCGUIRE ASKS A QUESTION FOR HER SON DAOUD (age 3): He asked about where we got him from and where we got his brother Joseph. He asked about death and if he would die and if he could take some pictures along with him. I said, "Go and ask Bawa. He will give you the best answers."

BAWA MUHAIYADDEEN: The children of today ask very subtle questions. We did not ask such questions at their age.

Today, this young child asked, "Where did I come from? Where did my brother come from? Where do we go when we die? Will I die? What is death? What will happen?" These are the questions he is asking.

Although we have matured and attained a certain state, we have not thought about the questions today's young children are asking. If we had reflected upon these matters, we would have analyzed our own affairs and progressed much farther.

The things this child has thought about in his three years, we have not thought about in our thirty, forty, fifty, or sixty years. We have to wonder, "Through whom is God teaching us? Through whom is He warning us?" It is through these children. Through them God is reminding us about these important matters concerning life itself. The questions this child asked contain the essence of what life is all about. We have forgotten, and God is reminding us through these children. Through them, He is explaining His history to us.

This is possible because little children live in a pure place. Their hearts are pure. Their unity and love are pure. Their faith is pure. When one cries, the other joins in and cries. When one laughs, the other joins in and laughs. When one plays, the other plays. When one walks, the other walks. When one falls, the other also falls. When one walks on all fours, the other does the same. Whatever they have they give to one another. They feed one another. Little children have pure hearts, pure qualities, and unity.

God is revealing these important matters to their hearts, but we adults have not reflected upon these things. If we had asked the same questions ourselves, if our hearts were like theirs, we would have discovered the answers by now, and we too would have the same pure love, the unity of the heart, and the peace they have. But we have not yet learned what these children have learned. How can we think of them as small? To a father, they are great. Their hearts are big. Their actions and love are very big. What don't they have? They don't have differences. They don't have the world in their hearts. They don't value the world; they only value God. Because of this state, their hearts are big, and they are thinking about these things. We must realize this.

This is why the prophets, like Jesus ☮, Moses ☮, and Muhammad ☮, said that if the adults do not come, at least send the small children forward. Why did they say this? Because the children are the family of God. They are the ones who have the wealth of God within them. Through these children, God reveals many things. We look at their questions as just the questions of small children, but they are asking what we have neither asked nor learned. By asking these questions, they are making us think about these things.

Are these children small? Their bodies are small, but their hearts are huge and so are the questions they ask. We are the small ones. We are small in wisdom. We have not learned what they have learned. In their love, in their hearts, and in their words, they are great. If we look intently at their words, we will see that God is revealing His history through them in many different ways. If we were to understand their questions, we would realize the great truths about God that are expressed within their words. These are not just small words, even though they may appear that way to us. These are words we have not learned, questions we have not asked our Father. Nor have we asked these questions in the world or even within ourselves. But these children are asking. They are inquiring into all this. Now look. See how Daoud is feeding his brother. If we had that kind of unity, we could understand many great explanations.

My brothers and sisters, my daughters and sons, we must reflect upon this. If we had such love and unity, what state would we be in? We would be God's babies. We would be talking to Him, and He would tell us about His matters. There is great learning in this.

If we would bring forth these questions from within ourselves, if we would ask about birth and death and what happens after we die, we would discover answers for ourselves. We would not be spending time with others or thinking about them. We would avoid wasting our time. May we search for this love, these good qualities, and this wisdom within our hearts. May we fashion these treasures within. Only if we search for this wealth can we discover ways of finding peace. I humbly request all of you to think about this.

My love you, my grandchildren. On a farm, cows or horses live together in large herds. If someone opens the gate and chases these animals out, they will run very fast on their four legs. However, if a man has fallen and is in their way, even though they are running so fast, the cows and horses will try to avoid him. They will pass without injuring him. Only if they panic and stampede might they trample him. You may have observed this. But, look at human beings today. When someone slips and falls, a crowd of people will trample right over him in an attempt to save themselves. They will just keep on running. This is the difference between man and animals.

Like this, in life, one person tramples on another and makes him suffer. Is this the state of a true human being? If we had inquired into the questions this small child asked, we would not behave like that. Human beings are doing what even animals would not do. Through animals, through trees, through babies, and through the wind, God is constantly revealing His history, His qualities, and His explanations. He is forever teaching through these different examples. We must think about this.

What comes through these children are great matters. The moment they are born and set foot on the earth, they know and speak all the languages God created. But we no longer understand them. We knew them earlier. We had learned everything when we first came here. We knew the languages of all the animals and birds.

What have we learned now? What we have been learning is not true knowledge. We have learned to kill, trample, and destroy others. If only we could remember the language we knew earlier, the language the children speak, we would not trample on one another. We would not cause others suffering. We would not hold on to the differences of race, religion, and color, or commit sins and kill others. Each child must reflect upon this.

We all have blood ties within us, and these cause our differences of race, religion, and color. These differences are circulating in our blood, keeping the unity of God buried in our hearts. We cannot perceive God's speech; it has been buried in our hearts. The unity of God and the unity of His duty, compassion, and love have been destroyed, and what is entrenched in our hearts now is darkness, desires *(nafs)*, illusion *(māyā)*, and *karma*.[1] These are what have come and settled there.

Our hearts have become dark. The heart itself has become the kingdom of darkness and is filled with the qualities of satan, the god of that kingdom. This god of darkness destroys the love and qualities of God's kingdom and establishes the kingdom of hell in our hearts. It destroys our lives and the lives of others. We must know this. We must realize that there are many secrets in the heart that explain the history of God and His kingdom. We must reflect upon this, remember the words we spoke when we were young, and bring that state of unity and love back into our lives.

If we can return to that state, then we can ask these questions and remember our Father's words. We will know the state in which we can speak with our Father again. But in order to have that connection to Him and be able to speak to Him or hear Him speak to us, we must establish that state. We must know His unity, love, peacefulness, compassion, and beauty. Then the beauty of our hearts and the beauty of God will become one. When that unity, purity, beauty, and speech enter our hearts, we will receive God's beauty and God's wealth, and His kingdom and wealth will be found within us. God's justice and prayer will enter us, and we will find innumerable treasures within. The wisdom and the ability to do this will be right there within us. That will be the kingdom of light, the kingdom of heaven. The kingdom of darkness will disappear. Hatred, differences, separations, anger, arrogance, the differences of the 'I' and 'you',

---

1. *karma* (T) The inherited qualities formed at the time of conception; the qualities of the essences of the five elements; the qualities of the mind.

karma, murders, sins, selfishness, differences of color and languages—all these aspects of destruction will disappear. We will know that which has no destruction. This state without any sin is God's kingdom. We will dwell as princes of God in His kingdom.

We must understand this. My brothers and sisters, every child, must understand this. We must realize our story. We must bring back and establish within ourselves what we knew earlier, when we were young. My grandson, you must realize this.

GAIL: He is getting tired. He has not slept all day.

BAWA MUHAIYADDEEN: This body feels tired, but God never feels tired. It is good to cut away the tiredness of the body. If you strengthen yourself with faith, then you will not feel tired. Strengthen faith and certitude within yourself. What is his name?

GAIL: Daoud.

BAWA MUHAIYADDEEN: Daoud is the elder brother and Joseph is the younger brother. Howard's children also ask all kinds of questions. Ahsiya and the other children ask many different questions that have a great deal of meaning. The questions Qadir asked when he was in Sri Lanka revealed so much inner history. What the child knew, the mother did not know. The secrets he knew, the mother did not know. The hearts of children are pure. Whoever has a pure heart is a child of God. Whoever does not have a pure heart is a child of satan, the leader of the kingdom of darkness, the kingdom of hell. We must think about this.

Daoud asked, "Where did we get our brother from?"

Daoud, you were once in the kingdom of heaven, the kingdom of purity where Allah rules. Allah is God. Your mother had faith in God, but she was wandering around in the world, in the kingdom of hell, so our Father and I came to this world and looked at her and thought, "How can we change this child and get her out of this kingdom of hell?" I reflected and said to our Father, "We have to give her something that will change her." That is why I asked God to send you to your mother first, Daoud. You were sent to teach her and to change her. In this way, she could realize and learn from you and leave this kingdom of hell. It is for this purpose that I asked God to bring you here from His pure kingdom, to your mother. But she still needed some more correcting, so then we called your brother also to come.

Now see, there are other children here. All these children were brought here to correct their mothers who had some faults. Many of these mothers had faults, and it was to correct them that you children were brought from His kingdom of purity. You have come as representatives of God to teach them, to teach God's secrets to your mothers, to teach them about birth and death, about the place you were before, and about the place you have come to. Mothers must listen and learn from their children.

Now, children, you must never forget these things. The reason you came from Allah was to teach your mothers, but you too must learn these things and not forget them. You must remember the answers to these questions. You must always remember these questions and remember the kingdom of the world, the kingdom of hell, and the kingdom of God. You must remember the kingdom of purity and the kingdom of impurity, the pure souls and the impure souls. You must always have the wisdom to understand these and continue to learn more about them. You must have the qualities and actions of God, our Father, and not forget His love, His unity, and His compassion. You must firmly establish the love and unity you have now and keep it for all time. You must always have that love, trust, compassion, and unity and try to keep it in you the way it is now. You must have God's qualities and God's wealth. You must always do this, without ever forgetting. Learn God's teachings and also learn about the world. If you learn and understand all this, you can finish the work you came for and leave. You will be able to go back to the place you came from, the place of your Father, the pure kingdom. Then you and your Father will be together in that kingdom where there is so much peace.

As you grow in your understanding of this unity and love, you will find the kingdom of peace within. You will find this beautiful kingdom of purity, peace, love, unity, and justice, and that is where you will live. In this kingdom you will understand the wealth of grace, the wealth of wisdom, the wealth of divine wisdom *(gnānam)*, the wealth of love, the wealth of compassion, and the wealth of patience. You will receive the pure wealth of divine knowledge *('ilm)*. God's undiminishing wealth will be yours. Your Father will give you His wealth and His beauty. When you receive all these treasures from your Father, He will give you the kingdoms of the three worlds: the kingdom of the soul, the kingdom of the world, and the kingdom of God. You will have limitless blessings of love and grace, in completeness. Children, you must understand this. You must not forget these questions or these explanations. This is how you must live. You must try to continue learning and living with this unity throughout your lives.

There was a prophet who was also named Daoud, (Prophet David ☮), who came long before you. He committed some mistakes, but then he asked for forgiveness. Now he is back again in God's pure kingdom. You also, with every breath, must ask for forgiveness whenever you do anything wrong. Daoud, do you understand? Then you will live in that kingdom of purity, both here and there. You will be forever praising *Allāhu* in this kingdom of purity. When you have a heart of purity, that is the kingdom of God. God will be in that kingdom of purity in your heart, and you too will be there. The body is a school, a big university. In this university, you must learn the answers to all the questions you ask. You must understand this. My love you.

Each one of you should work and learn like this and present the benefits of God's kingdom to me. Then I will have peace. *Anbu* (love), my grandchildren.

November 10, 1982

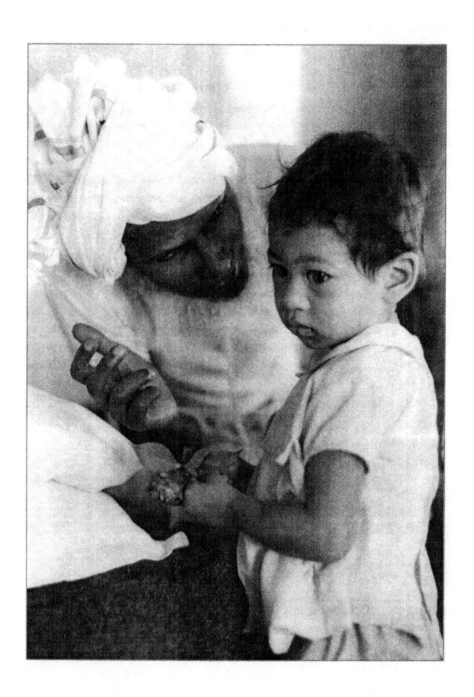

Session 5

What is the proper conduct between boys and girls ten years to eighteen years old?
31

I am ten years old and am wondering if it is proper to wear make-up.
32

What is wrong with dancing? Does that include ballet, tap, and dancing one does by oneself?
33

If we can't go dancing or play with boys, what can we do for fun?
36

How do we handle what our friends think about our Arabic names? People don't understand why we don't just go to a church or a synagogue like other people. How do we explain to them about the Fellowship?
37

If Adam and Eve had obeyed God, would the whole world still be a garden of Eden?
38

What does heaven look like?
39

If you go to hell, what feels the pain if you don't have your body?
39

Why did we choose to come here when we were already part of God to begin with?
40

Are there other people in outer space?
41

continued on next page

Session 5 *continued*

What should I tell my friends who told me God is
just pretend. What should I tell them?
43

What does Bawa mean when he says God was never born
and can never die? How did God come to exist then?
44

What type of Fellowship work can the children do
to feel a part of it?
46

Session 5

QUESTION: What is the proper conduct between boys and girls ten years to eighteen years old?

BAWA MUHAIYADDEEN: My love you, my grandsons and granddaughters, my brothers and sisters, my sons and daughters. There is a period in life when both male and female children are tempted to go on the wrong path. For girls this period is from about eleven to twenty-one, while for boys it is from fourteen to twenty-five. This is the time they have boyfriends and girlfriends. All the singing and dancing come during this time, and the qualities of love, lust, passion, sex, jealousy, falsehood, and deceit develop in them. The world, illusion *(māyā)*, the sixty-four kinds of sexual games, and four hundred trillion, ten thousand different kinds of qualities also come then.

If boys and girls are too close at a certain age, it is just like placing cotton next to fire. When fire touches cotton, it will burn and destroy it. Similarly, if during those years, these qualities touch boys and girls, their lives will be destroyed. The limit of their lives, their value, their potential, and their studies will be ruined. Wisdom and truth will be ruined. The unity with their parents and the love they have for them will also be ruined. They will be separated from them and burned before they are twenty-one years old.

At that age, many bad friends with many bad qualities will try to enter their lives, friends who steal, tell lies, and make love to one another, friends who deceive, destroy, and ruin other lives. If boys and girls with such qualities join together during these years, there will be a great deal of danger, and this danger will ruin their lives.

A girl is a very soft thing. She is beautiful, valuable, and very delicate. A girl is like a beautiful flower. If a beetle or some other insect falls on a flower when it is ready to bloom, it will nibble away at it. When a flower is damaged and no longer beautiful, its value is diminished. At this time the gardener has to be very careful and use insecticide to make sure the flowers are not eaten by bugs, so they will be valuable when the time comes to take them to market.

Like that, at this age you really have to use insecticide; otherwise, the bugs will jump on you and eat you. Your beauty, fragrance, and value will be diminished, and your market price will be lowered. Be very careful that this does not happen. Just as a gardener must make sure that a flower does not diminish in beauty or lose its fragrance, your parents who planted you and you children who are the flowers, the roses, have to be very careful. It is at this time that all the beetles and insects will climb on you and try to destroy you. A beetle that sits on a flower is not just going to sit there. It is coming to eat you. That is absolutely certain. As you mature a little more, you will have to be very careful. You need to know that any beetle who comes near is coming to eat you. It did not come to be your friend. You can be very certain of that. You must be aware of this and understand it. That is why boys and girls must be very careful with each other. It is like keeping cotton and fire in the same place. It is not good for boys and girls to get too close.

QUESTION: I am ten years old and am wondering if it is proper to wear make-up.

BAWA MUHAIYADDEEN: My love you, jeweled lights of my eyes. If a flower paints itself, its original, natural beauty will be ruined. Why would God create it as a flower if it needed make-up? It is already beautiful and fragrant, and it does not need any make-up.

There is no one, not even a ghost, who will not be enchanted by a beautiful girl. Even an old man who is about to die will be entranced by her when he looks at her. God gave women such natural beauty. He gave you that beauty already, and it is good for you to keep it beautiful. Your wisdom, qualities, and love will be so much more beautiful if you keep them natural. God gave you this natural beauty as a beneficial gift, so you do not need to put make-up on it. That would be like painting gold. Paint covers the beauty and hue of the gold and keeps it from shining.

Who needs make-up? Not you. Only old ladies need make-up, wrinkled old ladies who have done all their dancing and acting and whose nerves are wasted and bones about to dissolve. They are the only ones who need make-up. There are even some old men and women who still desire the world and still want to act and dance, so they need to go for plastic surgery to smooth out the wrinkles in their skin. But God has given you the gift that is appropriate for your age. Therefore, I do not think you need to use make-up.

QUESTION: Bawa has said it is not good to go dancing. What is wrong with that? Does that include ballet, tap, and dancing one does by oneself?

BAWA MUHAIYADDEEN: My love you, jeweled lights of my eyes. Your questions are very amazing. The person who has to answer them will also have to be amazing. Very well, I will tell you.

Everything in the world is dancing and music. Look at an oak tree. How much music it makes and how it dances when the wind blows! Raising its branches, it dances with each breeze. Every single branch dances so beautifully. Oak trees dance like this. Leaves, flowers, trees, and bushes all dance to music. They all take part in the drama.

When you stand by the seashore, you can watch the waves of the ocean dance, rising up with the sound, "Ooosh!" and coming down with the sound, "Ooooh!" Everything you see is an actor, and you can watch the music and drama God created. This drama exists in everything. But is that all there is to it?

My love you. Look at how your mind dances inside you, how each thought in your mind dances with the sixty-four kinds of arts and sexual games. But what enjoyment have you found from that? You have watched the ocean and the trees dance. You have watched the drama in the world, and you have heard its music. And yet you have still not seen the point of it all. What is the melody? What is the song? What is the meaning? What point does it make? You have not really looked into these things. But once you understand, you will realize the drama that exists not only in the ocean, on land, in the jungle and the city, but also in the mind, inside the body, and within life itself. Everywhere you look you will see drama and dancing.

Illusion does not just exist outside; it is inside too. Dancing is not done only on the outside; it is going on inside too. The dance you perform in the night is what you see outside, in the daytime. When you finish all the sexual games of the night, they become the daytime dances and dramas. But these are just sexual games. The things that people do in the darkness become the dramas they act out later in the light. What is in the mind dances within you at night, but then in the daytime these thoughts dance on the outside and become the act you put on. We are all actors. Everyone is acting.

However, if you are wise, you will understand the meaning of the act. With your wisdom, you will discover the meaning in it. You will understand its beauty, its value, its happiness and sorrow, and its outcome. Think about this and realize that this kind of dancing and acting takes place on both the inside and the outside. You need to understand this with your wisdom.

A tree sways to the music of the wind, but a strong wind can break off a branch, and an even stronger wind can topple the whole tree. The waves of the ocean can break down the shore, but a tidal wave can destroy a whole city. Like that, if the mind sways too much, it can make your blood pressure rise, and when it rises too high, it can cause a nervous breakdown.

Therefore, look at the cause behind each thing and know what the result will be. Know the point, the meaning, the state, and the outcome of this acting and dancing and drama. Understanding this is very important. If, with wisdom and good qualities, you understand with clarity, then you will never go dancing, because you will see that it is just an art that comes from the mind and from the dog of desire and the torpor of illusion. You really need to correct this in yourselves.

You should ask yourself, "What is the dance between me and God? What is the dance between me and the truth?" That is the kind of dancing you need to understand. What is the connection between the soul and God? He watches and you dance. Wisdom dances and He watches. Love embraces and both are in unity. That is the kind of dance you have to dance, with wisdom.

You can make God love you through the beauty of your qualities. You can enchant all lives through truth. It is this kind of acting that all lives will praise. Kings, beggars, birds, snakes, four-legged animals, and poisonous beings will all come to pay their respects to you. This is the kind of praiseworthy acting you should do. This is the kind of dancing that will make demons, ghosts, and devils run away, but it will draw human beings and all good beings closer. They will come and pay respects to you. This is the kind of dancing you do all by yourself. It is a very good thing to do.

Only when doing this kind of dance do you dance alone. In all other dances, you are dancing with the sixty-four sexual games, the sixty-four arts, the four hundred trillion, ten thousand 'spiritual'[1] qualities, the five elements, and the desire for earth, woman, gold,[2] and illusion. You will not be dancing alone then.

The only dance that will heal all the sorrows of your birth is the dance done completely alone. This is the dance you must do. It is the highest art of dancing, and it can end all your sorrows. If you can dance this dance, it will be very good. But, just like everyone else, you are trying to dance with the five elements. That is useless. What is the use of a tree dancing? Either some of its branches will break or it will fall to the ground altogether.

This world is just a stage we dance on, and all of us are actors. Who is going to get the prize? Even tiny newborn babies want to win the prize. Look at this little child called Ummul Khair. Even she comes here to dance. Ahsiya and 'Abdul Ghaffur also come and dance right in front of us. They are only little babies, and already they are dancing to win a prize.

From newborn babies to old men and old women, all are dancing to receive a prize. Everyone is an actor and is dancing and praising himself, saying, "Ah, my dance is the best! How is my act?" But since everyone came to dance, who is left to watch? And who is left to award the prize? There is no one watching. So you can never win a prize. There is just you, yourself, doing the dance and praising yourself. Then you grow tired and remove your dancing clothes, and it's over. That is useless.

However, true dancing has a use. If you dance alone, in the way

---

1. 'Spiritual' qualities: 'Spiritual' is a word Bawa Muhaiyaddeen uses to mean 'not tangible or material,' i.e., in the nature of a spirit or spirits. Thus, every thought-form is a 'spiritual' form.

2. Bawa Muhaiyaddeen refers to the three desires for earth, woman, and gold, the explanation being desire for land, sensual pleasures, and wealth.

I told you earlier, then God will give you the prize of paradise. He will give you the prize of life. He will give you a heavenly life here, a prize of peace, a prize that will make all lives bow before you. God alone will watch that dance and give the prize, because that is the good dance, the good act. So, dance that dance with His qualities and then receive His prize. That will be good. My love you.

~~~~~

QUESTION: If we can't go dancing or play with boys, what can we do for fun?

BAWA MUHAIYADDEEN: I was just telling you about how to be happy and have fun. Once upon a time, a man was thinking, "If I wrap my backside in a loincloth made of gold, my backside will be very happy and peaceful." And his backside was also thinking, "I need peace. If you wrap me in gold, I will be peaceful."

So the man said, "Okay, let my backside be peaceful," and he wrapped it in a golden loincloth. Suddenly everything he ate turned into gas. If he could have gone to the bathroom, it would not have smelled so bad. But because he was wearing this golden cloth, he was holding it all inside.

Finally, he could not control himself any longer. The urine, feces, blood, and smell all came out onto the golden loincloth. In the end, neither the backside nor the cloth ever found peace. The loincloth was very dirty and said, "Yuk! This didn't give me peace. There's nothing more disgusting than this! If I had stayed in a place where gold belongs, I could have retained my value. There is nothing more disgusting than sitting on this backside."

This is what it is like if you decide to go dancing with boys and try to have fun in the world. It will be just like what happened to the loincloth. If, however, through your own wisdom, your qualities, your clarity, and your faith in God, you try to find peace inside yourself, then that will be true peace.

The backside thought it would find peace by wearing a golden loincloth, but the stench was unbearable. Finally, the loincloth shouted, "Let me go, let me go!" Also, it was making the man's backside itch, and he kept scratching and scratching. Finally he went to a public bathing place, took off the loincloth, and scrubbed himself. Then the backside said, "I don't want this loincloth anymore. It's too itchy." So the man left it there and went away.

Then a man who had oozing sores on his backside came along. He wanted to take a bath, but he had no loincloth. Seeing the golden loincloth lying on the ground, he put that on and went to bathe. After his bath, he too took it off and went away. Next a man with another disease came and used the loincloth. He too left it behind and went on his way. After that, a man with a venereal disease came along and put it on.

In this way, one after another who came to the public bathing place put on the loincloth. And in the end, neither the backsides nor the loincloth ever found peace. Even though it was golden, the loincloth did not find peace, because it had to put up with all the foul smells. It thought, "If I had stayed on the backside of just one person, I would have only had to put up with his smell. But since I left him and came here, I have had to experience all the evil and *karma* of the world from the backsides of so many different people. I never found any peace. I now realize that if a loincloth decides to go to another place, it can only end up on another person's backside.

That's the way it is when you try to find peace in the world. If you think, "Instead of just staying here, if I could go out and have some fun, I would be peaceful," you will experience what the golden loincloth did. If you try to find peace by going to other places in the world, you will have to get onto everybody's backside. No matter how much make-up you put on, and no matter where you go hoping to find peace and tranquillity from the world, your mind and desire will give you a foul smell. The stench that comes from your thoughts will never give you peace.

Therefore, none of these things are of any use. What you need to make yourself beautiful and peaceful exists right within you. That clarity is within you. You do not need to search for it from others or from the world. It cannot be found outside. Find what it is within— that will give you peace. Find the state of wisdom, good qualities, love, faith, and trust. That is what will give you peace.

QUESTION: How do we handle what our friends think about our family having Arabic names? People don't understand why we don't just go to a church or a synagogue like a regular family. It's hard to explain to them about the Fellowship. Can Bawa tell us how to deal with this problem?

BAWA MUHAIYADDEEN: My love you. Tell this to your friends. Ādam and Hawwā' are Arabic names. Adam and Eve is what they are called in English, and Sakthi and Siva is what they are called in Tamil. Allah is an Arabic name. God is an English name. Kadavul is a Tamil name, and Yahweh is a Hebrew name for God. These are just names.

Noah is called Nūh in Arabic, while Noah is the Christian name. Ibrāhīm is an Arabic name, and Abraham is the English version. Ismā'īl is an Arabic name and is equivalent to the English name Ishmael. Mūsā is an Arabic name and Moses is the Hebrew and English name. Dāwūd is the Arabic version of the English name, David. 'Īsā is an Arabic name, and Jesus is the English name. We say Idrīs and Muhammad in Arabic, as well as in English. We say Ishāq and Ayyūb in Arabic, and Isaac and Job in English. Yūnus is an Arabic name, and Jonah is the English equivalent.

What's in a name? There is nothing in a name. Whether the names are in the Bible, the Torah, or in the Qur'an, they are all the same. In Arabic, the mother of Jesus ☮ is called Sitti Maryam ☮, and in English she is called Mary. Sitti Fatimah is an Arabic name, and Mary Fatima is an English name. So what is there in all this?

There is only one point, one God, one truth, and one prayer. This is the truth. They are not separate or different. Tell your friends, "We go to the Fellowship because a church is there, a synagogue is there, a Muslim mosque is there, a Hindu temple is there, and wisdom is there. We go there to learn and to find the truth with clarity. Everything is there. Except for the Fellowship, all these things are only found in separate places of worship, but at the Fellowship we have them all in one place, and we learn about everything in unity. That is why we go there."

Do you understand? Just tell your friends that. Why should we talk too much about these things?

QUESTION: If Adam and Eve ☮ had obeyed God, would the whole world still be a garden of Eden?

BAWA MUHAIYADDEEN: Yes, the world might still be a paradise if Adam and Eve ☮ had obeyed God. If you continue to obey God, then the whole world will remain a paradise for you. If you do that, you will not lose paradise. If all the brothers and sisters obey God, then they too will live in paradise. Adam and Eve ☮ were forgiven for their faults, but if you do not start committing faults, and if you can establish that good state, then you will always live in paradise.

QUESTION: What does heaven look like?

BAWA MUHAIYADDEEN: In paradise everything that makes you sad is absent. Peace, love, and tranquillity are present. Paradise exists wherever everyone lives in unity. Everyone is in the same state, at the same level. That is paradise. Everyone is happy there.

In a flower garden many different colored flowers grow together. There are red and white flowers, roses, jasmine, and many fragrant leaves. All those colors in a flower garden make it very beautiful. Isn't that so? That is what a flower garden is like. When all the flowers of different colors live together, not divided into separate groups, it is very beautiful.

Like that, if all of you live together, no matter how many different colors you may have, it will be very fragrant, beautiful, and joyous. When all of you live as flowers do, when all of you are in that state, that is God's flower garden. That is paradise.

QUESTION: If you go to hell, what feels the pain if you don't have your body?

BAWA MUHAIYADDEEN: My love you. That is a mystery. When you sleep you have dreams, do you not? Many people have dreams. In them, you observe people singing, embracing, kissing, rolling around, flying, and sitting. You see all that in dreams. While your body is lying on the bed sleeping, another body is experiencing the dreams. That body travels to different places. You have all had dreams. You have seen them. Was it your body that had those dreams? No. That other body inside this body experiences the dreams. The outer body remains unmoving, while this inner body moves about and does things to fulfill and satisfy the thoughts of your mind. It is this inner body that suffers in hell.

When the physical body dies, you have to give earth's share back to the earth, fire's share back to fire, air's share back to air, water's share back to water, and ether's share back to ether. But the body within this physical body is the result of what your mind has created through your thoughts and desires. This is the body that goes to hell. The physical body is a house for you, but inside it is the second body, which you created with your evil thoughts. And there is yet another body—the body of the soul, the body of truth. This body is made from the qualities of God and your wisdom.

These three kinds of bodies do three different things. First is the physical body, which is a house God built for you out of earth. This body must be returned to earth and the elements. Second is the body made by your thoughts and your mind. This is what suffers in hell, and it is to this body that the questioning will come. Third is the body you prepare with your wisdom. If you fashion this body for the soul, the light of God will come there. This is the body that goes directly to God when you die. My love you.

※

QUESTION: Why did we choose to come here when we were already part of God to begin with?

BAWA MUHAIYADDEEN: That is a good question. The soul is a part of God and the reason you came here is to understand Him and to understand yourself. You came here to know what God is like and what you are like. You must know what God is, what you are, and what creation is. This world is a school, a university. You came here to this school to study God's secret and your own secret. God created this place so you could understand Him and know how mighty He is, and so you could understand yourself and all of creation. You came here to take the test and pass it.

Does a mother give birth to a child and then just keep it in the house? If you were kept home all the time, how could you understand the world and its many wonders? Your mother and father send you to school. Why? Because they want you to study, to learn, and to understand the world, yourself, and all the wonders. They want you to know what truth is. That is why your parents send you to school, and that is why schools were built. Your parents want you to understand things.

God did the same thing. He sent His children to this school so they could understand more about Him. There is the world of the soul, this world, and the world of the heart, which has within it eighteen thousand universes, paradise, God, and yourself. You have to understand all these. The world is an example. God is the Causal Creator of everything, the inner heart *(qalb)* is an effect, and you are the basic principle. From the example of the world, you are the basic principle that understands the causes within yourself and the One who is the cause of everything. You need to understand your Father. That is why you came here. Your Father sent you here to study. Just as your parents send you to school, God sent you to this world to learn about the eighteen thousand universes, this world, the world of the soul, the world of life, the world of wisdom, the world of divine wisdom *(gnānam),* the peaceful world of paradise, and the world of perfection, purity, and resplendence. He sent you so you could know your Father. This is just a school.

QUESTION: Are there other people in outer space?

BAWA MUHAIYADDEEN: There may be. But compared to all the people you have seen with your eyes, look at how many more people there are in your mind! So many thoughts arise constantly within you, and they are all people. And you don't know about all those people. In addition, how many people are there in your heart? And so many people exist within your five elements. So, no matter how many people you see on the outside, with your eyes, there are many, many more people inside you.

My love you. When you look into someone's eyes, you can see your own form reflected there. The eyes are a mirror in which you can see yourself. If you can become resplendent, like your eyes, and understand all that you see in the world, then you will be able to understand everything that exists. It is possible to see everything. Just as you see yourself in someone's eyes, if you can become shiny and resplendent like that, you will be able to see everything—heaven, hell, outer space, and the earth—all that is outside and all that is within you will be seen.

Once the eye of true wisdom and love (that vision that can see everything) opens within you and you understand the *qalb* (which is the pure kingdom of God, paradise), then you will be able to see all the eighteen thousand universes, the world of the soul, this world and the next, and all the people in them. But if that eye does not open, then all the things you see and all the words you hear will be only a dream. And just as in a dream, when you wake up, none of it will remain.

Only when the eye of wisdom opens and that state comes to you will you understand and see what you have to see. Until then, can we tell you what it is like? No, we cannot tell you about the secrets of God, nor can we show you by giving examples. Science, research, ignorance, and false wisdom can be learned through examples, but the secrets of God cannot be known that way. But you will know everything for yourself when true wisdom comes to you and that inner eye opens. At that point you will see that people in heaven exist here and people here exist in heaven. And people from outer space can be seen on this earth and people on earth can be seen in outer space.

If a plane leaves the United States and travels thirteen thousand miles, visiting many countries, is the plane still here after it has left? No, the plane follows its various routes and then returns. Similarly, you can see people in outer space on the earth and people on the earth in outer space. It is all just a journey. It is like a plane going and coming. If you have the wisdom to see, then you can easily know where the journey leads. You must search for that wisdom.

You are not very far away from God, nor are you far away from paradise. This world, hell, and heaven are also not far from each other. You can see them all within yourself. The fifteen worlds can be seen inside. There are seven worlds above and seven worlds below. The center world, your heart, is the world for your wisdom. It is also the world for earth, air, fire, water, and ether. Therefore, if you can understand that world in the center, then you can understand the seven worlds above it and the seven below. You need to understand this.

QUESTION: Two of my friends told me God is just pretend. What should I tell them?

BAWA MUHAIYADDEEN: Should you tell them anything? One day a person who was blind in both eyes was walking along a road, holding a light. A group of people who could see with both eyes came walking by. They bumped into him, broke his light, and knocked him over. Then they said, "You fool, are you blind? You have a light and yet you walked into us. Are you blind?"

He said, "Yes, I am. What you say is true. I have been blind from birth. I was carrying this light so others could see me and avoid me. My eyes cannot see. I can't tell the difference between darkness and light, so I wasn't holding this light so I could see, I was holding it so you could see me and avoid bumping into me. But even though you have eyes, you knocked me down and broke my light. Yet you call me blind.

"I don't need this light for myself. I carried it because I was afraid of you. What else could I do? Only a small number of people are blind. Most people can see, yet they bump into the blind people and make them fall. It's the people who can see that I'm afraid of, not blind people. We who are blind have a certain sense of balance and attention. We perceive things through feeling, awareness, intellect, and wisdom. On the other hand, people with eyes have lost their senses. Even though they have eyes to see, they don't use their eyes or their wisdom and so they are, in a sense, blind. That is why I am afraid and why I was holding the light. But you bumped into me anyway, so what else can I do? I can only say goodbye." Then the blind man walked off, tapping his stick.

Like that, each person acts in a way that fits the state he is in. He bumps against others, even though they carry a light, and then scolds them for what he himself has done. Even if they see a light approaching, such people will not step aside. They do not bother to check whether a person is deaf or blind. There are even people who are looking right at God and should have the eyes to see Him, but don't. So, it is foolish to try to teach ignorant people, or preach to them, or explain things to them by examples. We cannot show them anything.

What we can do is avoid such people. Take a different path than they do. Don't ever try to teach wisdom to someone who has no wisdom. Teach it only to someone who wants it. And don't try to teach someone who has no faith or determination. If you do, the wisdom you try to teach will only go to him and bounce back at you, just as weapons hurled against a rock bounce back at the one who threw them. What you give him might look like one thing to you, but it will look like something else to him. It might assume many evil forms in his heart and come back to hurt you in a number of ways. That is what happens when you try to teach wisdom to a man without wisdom. Don't try to teach people who are not searching and striving for God, or people who do not believe in God. Your effort will turn against you and become a dangerous weapon. Avoid people without wisdom. This is the advice given by some men of wisdom.

God is like a seed. Just as a seed needs to make a connection to the earth in order to grow, if you have a connection to His qualities, the seed of God will grow. But such people do not have the earth (of God's qualities) in which to grow the seed of God. So, instead of challenging a person's arrogance, it is better to avoid it. Just give a simple reply and then leave.

QUESTION: What does Bawa mean when he says God was never born and can never die? How did God come to exist then?

BAWA MUHAIYADDEEN: Some people will understand about God and some will not. God has no form, no shape, no color, no race, no religion, and no scriptures. He is not contained within any particular religious doctrine. He does not have the six evils. He has no wife, no child, no birth, no death, and no kith or kin. He has no house. There is no flag that flies for God. He has no ignorance or false wisdom. He does not have any jealousy, resentment, or vengeance. He exists here, there, and everywhere—within everything. He is life within life. He is light within wisdom. He is clarity within clarity. In the earth and in the sky, in the sun and in the moon, in the flower, in the honey, in the fruit, in life, in the body, in you and in me, He is the complete treasure. He is a power. That is God.

There is no place that He does not exist. There is nothing that

He does not see. God is a treasure that exists without ever having been created. There is nothing that He does not feed, and there is no time when He is not feeding some creation. He gives to all. He protects, watches over, and sustains. He is the unique all-pervasive Being who exists everywhere. He is *illallāhu,* the One who rules alone. He exists as a resonance, resonating in each heart.

He is the One who dispenses justice. He is the One who makes us aware of the state of conscience. Do you have a conscience? Does it show you what is right and wrong? When you do wrong does it say, "What you did was right," or does it say, "What you did was wrong. Say you are sorry. Go and ask for forgiveness."?

That is God. He is inside you, inside me, and inside everyone. He exists in feeling and awareness, warning us and giving us explanations. Such is the great treasure that is God. He is in a state of peace, tranquillity, serenity, compassion, unity, and perfection. He is not separate. He is the one treasure that dwells in all the lives of the one family. He is the One who is all-pervasive and supreme, the lone treasure resonating and resplending with the name *illallāhu.* Out of His many names, this is the name we have to understand in all its completeness. This is what is called God. Do you understand? Very few people realize this. Those who do understand this are very rare. The majority do not understand it. But people with wisdom, good qualities, and love, people who strive, who have the certitude and determination of *īmān,* and who have faith and clarity, can know this. Otherwise they cannot. Do you understand?

Razzāq, do you understand? Do you understand what Razzāq means? Do you understand whose name Razzāq is?[3] That is God's name. If you really become like Him and live in the way your name directs you to live, then you will know Him and know where He was born. He was born with you, He lives with you, and He will come and be with you. He will talk to you and explain to you. Without a shape or form, God exists in your life.

---

3. *ar-Razzāq* (A) One of the ninety-nine beautiful names of God; the Provider, the Sustainer and Maintainer; the Bestower of sustenance; the One who gives food to all creations according to the capacity and need of their stomachs. From the book *Asmā'ul-Husnā: The 99 Beautiful Names of Allah* by M. R. Bawa Muhaiyaddeen.

QUESTION: What type of Fellowship work can the children do to feel a part of it?

BAWA MUHAIYADDEEN: Before doing any other work, you should do all the work your mother and father need you to do. Do all the work in your own house. We all have duties at home. If you can do those properly, then you can come to do duty in the Fellowship. You can wash dishes if you like. You can help in the kitchen. You can take the trash out and help clean the house. You can clean the windows and clean all the dust brought in by the many people who come here.

You can be very loving to all the guests of the Fellowship. You can serve them. You can show excellent conduct and respect to all the people who come here. By your behavior, you can teach them how to trust other lives as much as their own. You can help them to realize these things by the duty you do. People will see what you do and then correct themselves. That is a very great duty. Give up your bad qualities and act with good qualities. Act like that. Do duty in that way.

We have a garden here. You can pull weeds and help plant things. You can also ask people who are working here if anything needs to be done, and someone can give you a job. You can say, "Please tell us if you need any work done." You can ask the house managers or the garden manager and do whatever job they give you.

It is good to do good work. There are several different kinds of duty. There is the duty that you have to God, duty to people, duty to the world, and duty to the *shaikh,* or *guru.* If you look very carefully to see what needs to be done and really try, if you do it with a face of love and a heart full of compassion, then you can do duty to everyone. You can do that both at the Fellowship and at home. That is the duty we must do. Do you understand? Do it just like that. *Āmīn.*

~~~~~

Precious jeweled lights of my eyes, today is your Saturday meeting. We students have gotten together and have reflected deeply upon things. We have shared them in this meeting of small children. Now, what must we find out from this meeting? What do we need to know? What is the truth? We must take these explanations into our hearts and our lives and act accordingly. We must really look deeply into ourselves and understand. We must have good thoughts, understand their good meanings, and try to nourish them within and make them grow.

Wisdom, knowledge, good qualities, justice, and fairness have to grow in your lives. Each of you must develop these in your own life. You should act in a good way and show respect to your mother and father, to everyone around you, and to your brothers and sisters. When you act in a good way, it will show everyone else how to behave like that, too.

To all your brothers and sisters, those who are here and those who are not, you must demonstrate these teachings by the way you act and the way you carry out your duties. Then people will look at you, correct themselves, and also start performing duty toward others. We have to show others through our own actions, not through words and talking. Mere talk is useless. We cannot preach to others. We cannot speak about religions. We cannot give them book knowledge or religious knowledge.

Our life itself is a huge book. There is a great story and a great secret right in our innermost hearts. We need to realize that each person has a book within himself. It contains stories about his life: the secrets of God, the secrets of the soul, the secrets of life in the world, and the secrets of life with God. That book is inside us. We must read that huge book and find clarity and explanations. We must understand what is exalted and what is low, what is true and what is false in life. We must understand the exaltedness of wisdom and the depth of ignorance. We must understand truth and falsehood, heaven and hell, and this world and the next. The history we have to understand exists right within us.

Precious jeweled lights of my eyes, each child needs to discover this in his own heart and analyze everything we have spoken about. After you have analyzed something, find the clarity within it and act in a very good way. Perform duty in your life. Learn more and more. Discover more and more secrets. You must try to do this. This is why we have gathered together here today. This is why we have had this meeting and this talk, and this is what we have to think about. This is the explanation of life, and these are the lessons we should learn. This is the progress we need to make. We must know what is exalted and what is low in our lives. Each child needs to reflect upon this. You and I must think and then try to act in the right way.

Precious jeweled lights of my eyes, my brothers and sisters, we must try to live our lives in unity, as one family, as one group. We must show the beauty and the complete wealth of that unity and give it again and again and again to all hearts. The way to do this exists within us, but it must come into our actions. We really must behave this way, because it is the right way.

The agitation of our minds is what causes the destruction of our lives. Our thoughts destroy us. Our minds create hatred for others. But it is not someone else that is your enemy, it is your own mind. The other person's mind is his enemy and your mind is your enemy. It is just the darkness of ignorance that makes you think another person's mind is your enemy or that your mind is his enemy. Your mind is your only enemy. Each person's mind is his only enemy. There is no other enemy. That is what will cause destruction. Think about this and reflect on it. Your mind points at someone else and tells you he is your enemy. That only hurts you and makes you suffer. If you think other people are your enemy, you start to blame them, and that is ignorant.

Some of you hold hatred in your mind and go to bars and drink to ease that. Some go dancing and try to forget. Some go to nightclubs, some to parks, some hang out on the corner, and some try to find peace at the seashore. But they will never find peace in those things. Peace only comes when a person overcomes the nature of his mind. If you go to a bar and become intoxicated, you will only become more and more stupid and feel more and more pain. That will cause trouble with your wife and children. It will cause more separation, more pain, more divorces, and more problems. That is not the way to solve the problem.

Get rid of the ignorance within yourself. Find understanding and peace within yourself. You must dispel evil, destroy ignorance, expand your wisdom, and find peace within yourself. That will bring certain victory.

Many problems, sufferings, sadnesses, and sorrows will come in life. The mind will bring them all. Your mind will bring enmity, hatred, doubt, suspicion, jealousy, pride; arrogance, *karma, māyā* and the three sons of *māyā (tārahan, singhan,* and *sūran);* the six evils of desire, anger, miserliness, greed, fanaticism, and envy; and the five sins which come later—intoxicants, lust, theft, murder, and falsehood. All these qualities can come. This is the nature of the mind. It sends these enemies to attack us. We project our own thoughts onto others, then we call those people our enemies. But it is these thoughts that cause separations and differences. They cause families to split apart. They cause enmity between people and between husbands and wives. They bring distress, sorrow, pain, and difficulties to our lives. It is these thoughts that do all this. The mind is really the only enemy, and we must overcome it. We must defeat it.

Are we going to find peace by going to a bar? Are those qualities going to be controlled by doing that? No, we have to control the quality of ignorance that is within us. We have to develop wisdom, love, trust, compassion, unity, and all the qualities of God. With our consciences we need to look at ourselves, analyze ourselves, perceive what the witness inside us is saying, and act accordingly. That way we can find peace. Otherwise, we will never find peace.

If we continue to follow the ways of the mind, we will just end up with suffering, pain, difficulties, suicides, and murders. We must examine ourselves with wisdom, change this state, develop the qualities of God, and try to achieve victory. This is the truth in life. Each child has to know this and try to understand it. Once you understand, you must try to make your lives clear, for by leading a clear life, you can find peace. When clarity comes, your life will be heaven, and peace will be your greatest wealth. This great wealth will create a paradise both in this world and the next. Your life will be a house of peace and tranquillity.

Each child, whether young or old, married or unmarried, the small children, the older children, the adolescents, and the newborns have to think about this. Each child has to reflect upon these explanations and try to understand them.

Precious children, each one, whether you are learned or unlearned, whether you are a teacher, a doctor, a poet, or an engineer, whether you are rich or poor—whoever you are, this is the way to attain peace. This is how we can learn about the house of peace. We can never attain peace by obtaining titles or honors. We need to have *sabūr* (inner patience), *shakūr* (contentment), *tawakkul* (giving all responsibility to God), and *al-hamdu lillāh* (giving all praise to God).

Inner patience is very necessary. When things become more difficult, we need to be content, and when things become even more difficult, we need to give total responsibility to God and say, "I can't do anything. Only You can do this." And if things become still worse, we should place our trust in God and say, "This is Your responsibility. *Al-hamdu lillāh.* All praise belongs to You." We need to make our hearts strong. Then we can find victory.

Precious jeweled lights of my eyes, each child, these are the lessons you and I must learn. People with wisdom are great people, even if they are young. Whether you are young or old, it is wisdom that makes you great. People without wisdom are small, even if they are very old. You may be a king or call yourself a great *gnāni* (wise man), you may possess many titles and honors, you may be anything, but if you do not have the explanation of truth and wisdom, you are a small person. People may be older in years than you are, but you can be older in wisdom. For wisdom there is no age.

The love, the qualities, and the compassion of God belong to everyone. One who has the plenitude of these qualities will be considered a great one in love and wisdom. But if you do not have love and good qualities, then no matter how old you are, you will be considered small. These qualities do not belong to any particular age.

Each child must reflect on this and open the way to the truth. Each child must learn and try to understand and achieve victory. We must strive to do this in our lives. *Āmīn. Āmīn. As-salāmu 'alaikum wa rahmatullāhi wa barakātuhu* (May the peace and blessings of God be with you). May God help us all.

April 23, 1983

Session 6

How did Bawa get so wise?
53

If God has no beginning or end, how did He get here?
53

At what age do you think boys and girls should date,
and at what age can boys and girls leave home?
55

Is rock and roll bad for you?
55

How does the heart move? And why can't you see the angels?
56

Why did God make satan if He wanted us to be good?
57

How can God be in everybody's heart if He is only one?
57

How do you know what people are thinking?
58

How can I go to Mecca?
59

Why has God chosen for satan to be evil?
60

Session 6

ILMI MUHAIYADDEEN (age 5): How did you (Bawa) get so wise?

BAWA MUHAIYADDEEN: My father, the father of my soul taught me. And now, my Ilmi Muhaiyaddeen, the father of your soul is teaching you. Because I listened to what the father of my soul said and obeyed him, wisdom came to me. So, if you listen to all the words of the father of your soul, the way I did, and obey them and act in a good way, wisdom will come to you, too. Do you understand? Good. Are there any other questions?

DANIEL ISHMAEL (age 11): If God has no beginning or end, how did He get there?

BAWA MUHAIYADDEEN: If God has no beginning or end, how did He get here, right? That is a good question.

The beginning is a limit and the end is a limit. Anything created has a beginning and end. Thus everything God created—the world, the sun, the moon, and the stars, 'you' and 'I'—all have those limits. They have to start and they have to end. When they reach a certain limit, they are finished; they do not live any longer.

But the power that is God has no limit. Why? Because God has no beginning and no end. He is the owner of everything that has a beginning and an end. He owns the kingdom of the world and all the other kingdoms. God is the king. He is the king of the soul. He is the One who creates all the souls, nourishes them, and then calls them back again. He is the owner of everything, the master, the wise man, the father. He is the poor man and the rich man, the king and the beggar. He does all the work but He cannot be seen. He is a naturally existing treasure. That is why He will never perish. He cannot be destroyed.

What is God? God is good qualities. God is pure wisdom. God

is good thoughts. God is justice, the One who gives true justice. God is truth. He is the One who gives you peace within, every second. If you ask a pure question, He answers it. If you request something bad, He answers that, too. If you ask one way you will get an answer that is beneficial for you, but if you ask the other way the answer will be one that leads to ruin. The answer you receive will be appropriate for the state you are in.

My love you. God has no end. He is a mysterious power. He is the owner of everything. He has no form, no shape, no self-image, no color, no hue, no bigotry, and no differences. People call Him by many names. People call four hundred trillion, ten thousand 'spiritual' things God. They call him sun god, moon god, water god, air god, and countless other kinds of gods. They even call cows or dogs or donkeys or horses God. Whatever they worship, they say, "O God."

Some people call Him God. Some call Him Yahweh. Some call Him Allah. But in the end, truth is what a person who has wisdom will discover. He will realize that God is truth, a treasure of great mystery. When you understand the truth and the mystery, you will realize what God is. He is a naturally existing treasure. He was never created. Once you see Him, you too will become natural. When you become natural, you will not be destroyed. If you join with Him and if you stay with Him, you will not be destroyed.

God is a natural treasure. He will exist forever. Everything else will change. But we do not fully know what He is yet. We are still learning. We have discovered only a small amount about Him. But, you come with me, Danny, and then, later, I will tell you about everything I have discovered. If you come with me, you will understand. But you have to give up your naughtiness and stay close to me.

If I am going along and you straggle behind, you may break your arms and legs, and you will have to go to the doctor. You must stop all this and follow me with very good conduct. You have to watch me closely and stop breaking your arms and legs. If you do come, you will understand. You will know the point. Will you come with me?

DANIEL ISHMAEL: Yes.

BAWA MUHAIYADDEEN: Okay. Then we will go.

AISHAH SHAHIDAH SIMMONS (age 13): I have two questions. I want to know at what age you think boys and girls should date, and at what age can boys and girls leave home?

BAWA MUHAIYADDEEN: That is a very good question. Whenever your parents find you a husband, you can leave home. Then you can date. You can go to the movies with him. Until then, anybody you go out with will ruin you. They will destroy your value, your life, and your dignity. Do you understand? Good.

Any more questions?

LOU WILSON ASKS A QUESTION FOR HIS SON JONAH (age 6): Jonah has a question, but he is too shy to ask. It is not a wisdom question. It is a practical question. Is rock and roll bad for you?

BAWA MUHAIYADDEEN: It is worse than the feces that goes into the toilet. At least feces gets burnt to ashes and can be turned into fertilizer. Rock and roll is absolutely useless. It just ends up in hell. It takes you to hell.

Therefore, it is no good. Jonah, do you understand?

JONAH: Yes.

BAWA MUHAIYADDEEN: Do not think about rock and roll. Just learn wisdom.

All right, little children, quickly ask your questions. Ask anything you want to.

RAHEEM BATH (age 4): I don't know what my question is. I don't know.

BAWA MUHAIYADDEEN: Okay, then your name is more than enough. You told us your name. That is good. Raheem, right? Raheem Bath, *as-salāmu 'alaikum* (May the peace of God be upon you). Your name is really good. We are happy you told it to us.

Does anybody have a question?

QADIR STERN (age 4): How does the heart move? And why can't you see the angels?

BAWA MUHAIYADDEEN: Good son, my grandson. How does the heart move? The heart moves because of six things: earth, water, fire, air, ether, and the soul. These are the six lives. Earth is Adam, water is the Angel Michael, fire is the Angel Israel, and air is the Angel Israfil, may the peace of God be upon them all. The fifth is ether, which is the mind, *māyā*, and color. It is the workings of the mind. And the sixth is the pure soul *(rūh)*, which has the wisdom of truth. Earth, water, air, blood, fire, heat, colors, *māyā*, and thoughts, and the pure soul are all within your heart, and they are what make it move.

The good thing, God's treasure, is the pure soul of man. Earth, air, fire, water, and ether are impure souls. Both the pure soul and the impure souls move. The five lives are mingled together in the earth and the sky, but the pure soul is mingled with God. When you understand these two areas, you will see that the angels are there. Satan is there too. He is in your mind and in your bile.

Wisdom and the soul take their food from Allah. Wisdom gives the true explanation for everything. When you acquire wisdom and discover God and the soul, when you understand what things your wisdom must look for, and when you know yourself, the angels and all the other things within you can be known. The angels will be there. Hell will be there. Heaven will be there. God will be there. And you, your soul, will be there. Everyone will be there. Once you discover that, you will understand.

When you search for wisdom and God's qualities and after you cut away all the things that are wrong, then you will be able to take what is right and do what is right. Then you will understand. Do you understand, Qadir?

QADIR: Yes.

BAWA MUHAIYADDEEN: Then you can become a human being. *As-salāmu 'alaikum* (May the peace of God be with you).

QADIR: *Wa 'alaikumus-salām* (May the peace of God be with you, too).

RABIATHUL ADAVIYA SHABNAM MACAN-MARKAR (age 7): Why did God make satan if He wanted us to be good?

BAWA MUHAIYADDEEN: That is a very good question. God wants us to be good, so why did He create satan?

Originally God created satan as a good one. In the heavens, satan was the ruler of the jinns. But when God created Adam, man, as an exalted being, satan became jealous. Adam was created out of earth, and satan was created out of fire. Because of that, satan had anger, and when he became angry he became satan. He had anger, jealousy, and feelings of vengeance. First came anger, then jealousy, and then doubt entered him. He started thinking, "I was created out of fire and Adam was created out of earth. So, how can he be better than I am?" Since he thought he was better than man, satan filled up with pride, and became really hot. That was when he turned into satan. God did not create him as satan. It was when his qualities changed that God said, "You are *mal'ūn*, the one who strayed from the path," and cast him out of heaven into hell.

Do you understand? God did not create satan the way he is now. Satan created himself. Bad qualities are satan. If he gives up those bad qualities, he will no longer be satan; he will be just another jinn. It is like that with human beings, too. Whenever they acquire those bad qualities, they also become satan. But if they do not have pride, anger, envy, doubt, vengeance, lies, treachery, deceit, and selfishness, they can be human beings. If satan gives up all his bad qualities, he can be a jinn again. If a man has satan's qualities, he will be satan, too, but if he gives up those bad qualities, he can be like God. He can be a representative of God.

Do you understand? God did not create anyone as satan. He created only good beings. He created everyone good. Each person can choose what he wants. When a man chooses things that are bad, that changes him into a bad person, and he starts to do bad things.

Do you understand? My granddaughter, much love to you. My love you. *As-salāmu 'alaikum* (May the peace of God be with you).

AHSIYA POSNER (age 6): How can God be in everybody's heart if He is only one?

BAWA MUHAIYADDEEN: Good. Ahsiya, my love you, my granddaughter. My love you, Ahsiya. That is a very valuable question. What Shabi asked and what you asked us now are very good questions, very great questions. My love you, jeweled light of my eyes.

Do you see the light bulb in this room? You can see it, can't you? You can also see the street lights along the road and the lights in your house, can't you? Wherever you turn on a switch, the light comes on. Light is light. It is the same everywhere, whether it is in this room or in your house.

In the same way, there is one power that is God. He is the motor. All the souls came from that motor, from His miracle. The souls are rays of light, like lighted bulbs. God is the power, and all the lights came out from Him. Just as a current goes throughout all the wires [in a city], the power of God also goes everywhere. But you have to turn on a switch to make the light come forth. Like that, you must make God's qualities, wisdom, actions, and truth function within you. Then the light of God will shine in you. Every house has light bulbs, and the current goes everywhere, but it is up to you to turn on the switch. Then there will be light in the house. Similarly, everyone can have the light of God in them if only they turn on the switch that brings God's qualities into action. Do you understand? My love you. *As-salāmu 'alaikum* (May the peace of God be with you).

MELISSA D. BROWN (ZAHARA) (age 11): How do you know what people are thinking?

BAWA MUHAIYADDEEN: That is a good question, too. When you comb your hair or put on powder, you look at yourself in a mirror, don't you? Does the mirror see it or do you see it? Do you see it or does the mirror see it? Like that, if you go to your father, a man of wisdom, he will see you and you will see him. He will show you your faults, so you can correct yourself. He is a mirror. He shows you things so you can correct yourself and make yourself better.

When you stand in front of a mirror and look at yourself, the mirror tells you where your hair needs to be combed or your shirt needs to be straightened. It is like that when you go to a man of wisdom. He shows you what is inside you. He says, "Comb this part here. Act this way and not that way." Do you understand? This is what you have to discover. To a man of wisdom, your heart is a mirror, and he can see everything in it.

Thank you. My love you.

BASEER AHAMED MOHIDEEN RIZA MACAN MARKAR (age 6): How can I go to Mecca?

BAWA MUHAIYADDEEN: Are you going to Mecca? You went from Ceylon to London, from London to America, and now you want to go from America to Mecca. From Mecca, where will you go?

BASEER: I'll go to Ceylon.

BAWA MUHAIYADDEEN: Ask Araby. She has the *dunyā* (the world). It is Araby's *dunyā* birthday today. You are her grandson. You have a father. You need a lot of money to go to all those places. You cannot go on a journey without money. When you were sick, they spent a great deal of money to make you well. They even sold some land to get money. They spent close to a million *rupees*[1] on you. Think about this.

You do have to go to Mecca on *hajj* (holy pilgrimage).[2] There is one way that Mecca will come looking for you and another way that you go looking for Mecca. If you want to go to Mecca, you need to spend money, but if Mecca comes to you, you do not need any money. If you strive hard, Mecca will come to you.[3] To go to Mecca in this way, you need your wisdom, your *īmān* (faith, certitude, and determination), and your love for Allah. If you spend those things, and if you spend all your prayers and worship, then Mecca will come to you. But to go to Mecca (physically), you have to earn money.

All right, if you like, you can go. Ask your father and mother.

---

1. *rupee* (T) A unit of money in Sri Lanka and India.
2. *hajj* (A) The holy pilgrimage to Mecca in Saudi Arabia. It is the fifth *fard* (obligatory duty) in Islam. The inner *hajj* is to enter the state of dying to the world, even before the body dies.
3. Bawa Muhaiyaddeen refers to the Mecca within the heart of man.

Ask your grandfather and everyone. There is one *hajj* to be done while you are alive. You can go. Do you understand?

Wherever you are, you have to look for Allah. That is what you should do. Just because you go to Mecca or you were born in Mecca does not mean you will go to heaven. Abū Jahl[4] and all those bad people were born in Mecca, but they never went to heaven. The dogs, foxes, and horses that are born in Mecca do not go to heaven. Only someone with *īmān*, with the wealth of faith, can go to heaven. Do you understand? So strengthen those things.

If you like, you can go to Mecca at the time of *hajj*.

For two or three days now, you have not seemed so energetic. What is wrong? Don't you feel well? Be happy. You are a very clever boy, very smart. How is your toothache?

BASEER: It's better.

BAWA MUHAIYADDEEN: He seems to have a cavity. When he has a toothache, he takes aspirin for it, by himself. He does that. He is a very clever boy. He is his own doctor. You might become a doctor someday. Okay, be happy. *Anbu* (love).

My love you, my children. What would you like? Do you have a question?

MICHAEL BIVINS (age 14): My name is Michael. You said, "God's will always comes true." If it is God's will for satan to be bad and for us to go to heaven and be with God, then if God did not want satan to be evil, he would not be evil. So why has God chosen for satan to be evil?

BAWA MUHAIYADDEEN: God never said that. He showed us good and evil. He said that one is on one side and the other is on the other side. If you go on the good side, that is what you will get, and if you go on the bad side, you will get that. You choose whatever you want. "I am the owner, and later I will give you what you asked for. If you want goodness, you can have that. If you want evil, you can have that." God said this in the beginning.

---

4. Abū Jahl: One of the foremost enemies of Prophet Muhammad ☮. His real name was 'Amr ibn Hishām, but the Muslims nicknamed him Abū Jahl, or the father of ignorance.

He showed us both sides and told us to choose. God said, "I have given you everything. You have to know what you want. Before you act, you have to find out what is good and what is evil, what is right and what is wrong. I will judge you according to the path you choose." Do you understand?

You have goodness within you and that comes from God. But you also have evil. God gave you both. He gave you this world and the next, and He gave you heaven and hell. Whichever side you choose is what you will get. The good or evil you receive depends upon what you choose. Do you understand?

MICHAEL: Yes.

BAWA MUHAIYADDEEN: All right. Thank you. *As-salāmu 'alaikum wa rahmatullāhi wa barakātuhu kulluhu* (May God's peace and blessings be upon you all). Precious children, jeweled lights of my eyes, may God always help you to go on the good path.

There is a great mystery known as life. When a jinn is put into a bottle, it no longer has a life of its own. Its life is imprisoned within that bottle, and its value, strength, and miraculous powers are lost. Man's life is like that. His value is imprisoned in the bottle of the five elements. The qualities of satan catch all the goodness in man, and he is imprisoned in a bottle. When this happens, his worth, the value of his wisdom, and the value of his wealth and freedom are destroyed. His life of peace is ruined. The qualities of satan catch man and put him in the bottle of the five senses, and his whole life is ruined. His freedom, strength, beauty, youth, the joy and freedom of youth, and the ideals of God, that light—all these leave him. The mystery of God's qualities and his strength decrease. He is imprisoned in the many thoughts his five senses bring him. Satan imprisons him in that bottle. He loses his freedom and his life is destroyed. In order for man to become free again, a man of wisdom must come and release him from the bottle.

A man of wisdom comes from God, as a messenger from Him. If satan imprisons you and makes you suffer, only a man of wisdom can remove the lid from the bottle with the key he holds in his hand. Then you can be free. You can escape. That is why you need a *shaikh*, a true *insān kāmil* (God-realized man). He must be a *shaikh* who can beat and chase away satan. He must be one that satan cannot approach, one that the fire of the jinns cannot come near or burn. Only such a *shaikh* can open the bottle and allow you to escape with your life.

Once you do escape, you have to change and give up your evil qualities and actions. You have to come to God's way. You have to go to a place where satan cannot go, a place where truth and God exist. If you do, you will triumph in your life. You will be free. Your life will be free. You will be very free. That is why you need a *shaikh*, a man of wisdom, a true man who can get you out of the bottle. He is the only one who can open it.

You have to reflect upon this with all your faith and trust. You should not have any doubt, suspicion, anger, or prejudice. You have to work very hard. You have to truly open your heart and turn and go on the straight path of God. This is certain to give you peace. If you have faith, certitude, and determination *(īmān)*, then wisdom will show you the straight path and you will find peace in your life.

Precious jeweled lights of my eyes, you must think about this. You must walk on that straight path. May God give you that help and that grace. *Āmīn. Āmīn. As-salāmu 'alaikum wa rahmatullāhi wa barakātuhu:* May it be so. May the peace and blessings of God be upon you all.

October 8, 1983

Session 7

Can Bawa give me a special prayer to say?

Session 7

MELANIE B. (age 7): Can Bawa give me a special prayer to say?

BAWA MUHAIYADDEEN: We cannot give you the highest prayer now because you are still young. There is a lot more you need to learn. You have to start slowly, and as you progress you will go higher.

The first prayer is: *Lā ilāha illallāh, Muhammadur-Rasūlullāh.* Write it down for her. (Bawa Muhaiyaddeen then repeats it slowly and in parts so the child can repeat it after him.) Take this as your special prayer.

Lā ilāha means: There is none other than You. *Illallāh* means: You are Allah. There is no god that can be compared to You or is equal to You. You have all power. You are the only One. You are the One who is alone. You are the One who made all of creation. You are the One who gives food to everything. You are the Father who protects all lives, the One who created everything, protects everything, and sustains everything. You are the One who causes lives to die and the One who revives those lives after death. You are the One who will ask the questions tomorrow [on the Day of Reckoning] about the right and wrong we have done. You are the One who gives judgment tomorrow. You are the only One; there is no god other than You. This is a small meaning of this prayer.

Illallāh. You are Allah. *Muhammadur-Rasūlullāh.* Muhammad ⊕ is Your representative. He is the Messenger from Your kingdom. He is the representative for Your entire kingdom of grace. He is the *Rasūl* ⊕, the wise man, for all the creations who are under Your gaze. You made him the *Rasūl* ⊕ through Your wisdom, You sent Your wisdom to his form. The *Rasūl* ⊕ is the form of Your wisdom and that is the light to *īmān*, to faith, certitude, and determination. For those who have faith in You, for those who have *īmān*, the *Rasūl* ⊕ exists as light. Through that light, he makes us know You and see You. Muhammad, the *Rasūl* ⊕, is Your slave, Your representative, Your wisdom, and Your power.

Lā ilāha illallāh, Muhammadur-Rasūlullāh. I follow and trust the Messenger that You have sent. I accept this truth of *īmān* and the truth of purity. Just as I accepted You, I accept Your representative, and I am setting out to reach You.

Give a copy of this explanation of this word to this child. There are many more explanations for this one word. There is so much meaning within it, but this is just one explanation for your *īmān*, your faith, certitude, and determination. *Āmīn.*

November 13, 1983

Session 8

Why is the world always hard?
69

Why can't we see the angels on our shoulders?
69

Session 8

MARY FATIMA WILLIAMS (age 5): Why is the world always hard?

BAWA MUHAIYADDEEN: The reason is because you and I have both grown old. You and I have become old in wisdom. Because the world has advanced through science, the mind of the individual flies away from God and the truth. Men are doing evil when they should be doing good. There are men who should be living like true human beings who have now set out to live like beasts. Man has lost his faith in God.

This generation does not live as good human beings in the state of true unity. They do not live with love. They do not consider other lives as valuable as their own or help others when they are in difficulty. When man acts, he forgets all such good thoughts. Because of this, the world has become hard.

It is the mind of man that experiences this difficulty. The world just looks on. The world a man keeps inside himself is what causes him difficulty. Each person finds the world he carries inside to be hard. But if man would keep the good treasures and the good world within him, he would find it very easy. Do you understand, Mary Fatima?

MARY FATIMA: Yes.

BAWA MUHAIYADDEEN: You have asked a deep question.

BAJEERAH LOWE (age 5): Why can't we see the angels on our shoulders?

BAWA MUHAIYADDEEN: That is a good question. Once we know what is good and what is evil, we will see them. When we understand good and evil and we are able to discard what is evil and do what is good, that is when we will be able to see them. Do you understand?

BAJEERAH: Yes.

April 18, 1984

Session 9

What should I say when somebody asks me what religion I am?
73

How does God take you to heaven or hell?
74

How did God make the first person alive?
75

Session 9

BAWA MUHAIYADDEEN: Ask your questions.

KABIRA MIRIAM HOCHBERG (age 6): What should I say when somebody asks me what religion I am? Everybody is asking me that.

BAWA MUHAIYADDEEN: Very good. Say, "I am *Saivam* (a Hindu). And if they ask you what *Saivam* is, say, "*Saivam* is purity." Then say, "I am a Christian." And if they ask you what Christianity is, say, "I follow the pure soul." Then say, "I am a Jew." If they ask you what that means, say, "It means to obtain release from the slavery in my life. Prophet Moses ☮ came to release the people from slavery. That does not mean to obtain freedom from a particular person but rather to be freed from all the things that enslave us in our life so we can reach that pure soul." Then say, "I am Islam." And when they ask you what Islam means, say, "Islam is unity. *Lā ilāha illallāh*. There is nothing else other than God. You are Allah, You are God. That is the *kalimah*. You affirm that there is only one God and have firm faith in Him."

Tell them, "Through Prophet David ☮, God united all four religions. Through Prophet Noah ☮, He brought about unity among the animals. He taught Prophet Jonah ☮ during the forty days he was in the stomach of a whale. God made people increase their faith in Him through Prophet Abraham ☮. Through Ishmael ☮ He taught them to perform *qurbān*¹ in order to sacrifice the desires and attachments that surround them. He sent Moses ☮ to release the people from the slavery that existed in their lives and to make them all one family. My religion is purity. To become free and to become

---

1. *qurbān* (A) Externally, it is the ritual method for the slaughter of animals, to purify them and make them permissible *(halāl)* to eat. Inwardly, it is to cut away the animal qualities within the heart of man, thus making one's life *halāl*. For a further explanation, see *Asmā'ul-Husnā: The 99 Beautiful Names of Allah* by M. R. Bawa Muhaiyaddeen, pages 180–184.

one family is Islam. One who understands all four religions is Islam.

"A person should study and understand each of the four religions in the correct way—*Zabūr* (Hinduism), *Jabrāt* (Fire worship), *Injīl* (Christianity), and *Furqān* (Islam and Judaism). If you look with understanding at the *Purānas,* the Bible, the Qur'an, and the Torah, you will see that everything is within the One. There is only one God, and everything is directed toward that one point. There are not different points. If you read all four scriptures, you will see that they say the same thing, and that one thing is all that remains in the end. Because people do not understand this, they say, 'This is my religion. That is your religion.' But the Prophet Muhammad ☉ explained that all five fingers have to be joined to pick up anything. His followers were like brothers and sisters."

Tell them, "I am in a group that brings all people together in unity. God said that when we go to Him we must go as one. I belong to a group that unites everyone, so I belong to all the groups.

"To know oneself is to know one's Lord. When my wisdom grows and when I know myself, I will attain that state."

You can tell them whatever you like. I still do not know what religion I belong to. I am still studying all four religions and trying to understand what lies at the end of each. In the process of studying them, I cry with those who cry, laugh with those who laugh, speak with those who speak, and learn with those who are learning. You must also do that. *Al-hamdu lillāh* (All praise belongs to God).

AHSIYA POSNER (age 7): How does God take you to heaven or hell?

BAWA MUHAIYADDEEN: My good daughter, my gold daughter, that is an excellent question. My love you.

You pick up an orange or an apple because you want to eat it, isn't that so? But what would you do if the apple or orange was rotten? You would throw it away, wouldn't you? You would not want to eat it.

In the same way, good things, such as truth, good qualities, and good wisdom are very tasty, and that is heaven. But bad qualities, bad intentions, and bad speech are not tasty. If you throw away these bad things, you will be in heaven. Hell will be gone; you will have thrown it away. Isn't that so? Do you understand? So throw away whatever is bad to your eyes, to your tongue, and to your wisdom. If something is bad, throw it away. Eat only what is good, the beautiful things. All right? Very good. May God protect you.

Any other questions from my daughters, my sons, my grandsons, and granddaughters? Any other questions?

IMRAN POSNER (age 6): How did God make the first person alive?

BAWA MUHAIYADDEEN: Let us wait to answer that until you grow up. First you must study hard. After that, you will get married and have children, won't you? At that time we will give you the answer to your question. After you create children of your own, we will explain this to you.

But for now, we will tell you this. In every matter, God can do whatever He wishes. For example, Jesus ☺ was born without a father. His mother, Mary ☺, did not have a husband. God created Adam ☺, the first man, without a father or mother. He was created from the earth. Eve ☺ was created from a bone, a rib, that came from Adam ☺. A woman did not give birth to her. Like this, in many ways God is capable of making something come into existence that was not there before and of taking away something that was already there. He can do that.

In the same way, when an intention arises in you, God is the One who fulfills it. As soon as you ask for something, God will give that to you. He brings comfort to your mind. If you are sad about something, He sees that and says, "My love you, my grandson. Go to Bawanga. Go see him and talk to him for a little while." And so you come here, and I give you chocolate. After that, I give you love. I speak words of love to you and change your state of sadness. Isn't that so?

IMRAN: Yes.

BAWA MUHAIYADDEEN: Exactly in the same way, God, too, gives us everything we need. Whenever we go to Him, He embraces and comforts us. He makes us happy. That is what God does for us. My love you. Do you understand?

All right, my children, please receive your candy on your way out. *Anbu* (love).

November 10, 1984

Session 10

What happened to Adam when satan spat on him?
79

When babies die, do they go to heaven or hell?
81

How do you get to God?
81

If you see God, do you see Him with your own eyes?
83

How do you destroy satan?
84

How did God destroy satan?
Can God destroy satan with His fire?
84

What happens to satan when he gets destroyed?
84

What happens when you die?
85

How do you get to hell or heaven?
85

Does satan take you to hell?
86

Session 10

BAWA MUHAIYADDEEN: *A'ūdhu billāhi minash-shaitānir-rajīm. Bismillāhir-Rahmānir-Rahīm.* (I seek refuge in God from the evils of satan, the rejected one. In the name of God, the Most Merciful, Most Compassionate.) *Allāhu ta'ālā Nāyan,* the Lord God, is almighty. May the One who exists in the central spot within your heart *(qalb),* within your chest, and within everything protect you, sustain you, and give you the wisdom and the abilities you need. May He give you the most exalted qualities and clarity, and may He protect you. *Āmīn.*

My children, my grandchildren, my granddaughters and grandsons, my sons and daughters, my brothers and sisters. Be the children of God and recite His names, so you can understand and resonate the sound, the resonance, of your Father. You must find the clarity to bring your lives to a good state and to reach a good place, so you can find the basic original treasure. To do that you need wisdom, the ability to use that wisdom, and good qualities.

My love you, precious jeweled lights of my eyes. If you have any questions, please ask, and if I know the answer I will tell you. If you do not have any questions, we can speak about other things. My love you, my grandsons and granddaughters, my brothers and sisters, my daughters and sons. Please ask.

KABIR GREEN (age 5): What happened to Adam ☉ when satan spat on him?

BAWA MUHAIYADDEEN: Ahamed Kabir, my grandson, what satan spat onto Adam ☉ was all his own bad thoughts, his evil ideas, his pride, his jealousy, his vengeance, his trickery, his four hundred trillion, ten thousand evil 'spiritual' thoughts, the arrogance of the 'I', and the quality of saying, "Only I exist. I am god!" Satan has such arrogant thoughts, and those evil thoughts are his hell. They are the spit that flows from the spring of his hellish thoughts. That is the worst of hells, and satan spat that poisonous hell onto Adam ☯. Now, when a snake bites a man, its poison spreads rapidly through him. The same thing happened as soon as the poison of satan's evil qualities fell on Adam's navel. It spread rapidly throughout his earth form. Even today satan's evil qualities develop within us much faster than God's qualities. Those qualities have been causing us harm ever since Adam ☯ was created. That is why so much evil comes our way and all kinds of poisonous thoughts arise within us, whenever we try to do even a little bit of good.

As soon as satan spat his evil thoughts onto Adam ☯, *Allāhu ta'ālā Nāyan* immediately called Gabriel ☯ and told him to remove that poison. Gabriel ☯ went to Adam ☯, and with two fingers pinched out the spit from the place it landed. But, even though it was removed and thrown away, some of his qualities had already entered into Adam ☯, and those qualities have been passed down from Adam ☯ to us.

My son, suppose we want to hit or attack someone but are unable to. That bad intention of ours will still try to enter that person to hurt him, attack him, or destroy him. And at the same time it will destroy us as well. When we are angry at someone or scold or attack them, or when we are jealous of someone, we are the ones who are hurt. We ourselves are hurt by the poison of the evil that exists in our own intentions, thoughts, and reflections. My love you. Such thoughts ruin mankind. Satan was sent to hell because of such thoughts. He suffered so much because of that evil. Those qualities and thoughts are what subject a person to hell, sin, evil, and suffering.

We have to change those bad qualities and acquire God's qualities, His actions, His beauty, His love, and His truth. God sent the prophets to us. He also sent wise men, people with faith and trust in God, and the lights of God, so we could cut away satan's evil qualities with wisdom and acquire good qualities and act accordingly. God sent the prophets so that the suffering satan underwent and the sorrow Adam ☯ endured would not come to us—so we could avoid all that. With trust in God and prayer to God, we must listen to the words of the prophets. We must listen to wisdom, study it, and attain clarity. Then we can know peace in our lives. We can attain the peace that enables us to give love to others. It was a small question but a big answer. Do you understand?

KABIR: Yes.

BAWA MUHAIYADDEEN: Yes. *Al-hamdu lillāh* (All praise belongs to God). Anything else?

AHSIYA POSNER (age 7): Some people die when they are born. Do they go to heaven or hell?

BAWA MUHAIYADDEEN: Good question. Is that Ahsiya? Ahsiya ☺ was a great lady in the world, a great saint. You also must become a saint in this world, a really great lady. God has to grant that to you.

My love you, my granddaughter. If little babies die or if young children die before they have reached puberty, they become *houris* (celestial beings). Up to the age of seven or ten, if the sins and the inherited evils and the illusion of the world have not yet touched them, and if bad thoughts have not yet touched them, they go to heaven. When children die in that state, they are called *houris*. They serve the heavenly beings and all the good people in the heavens, in the hereafter. They perform duty in this world as well as in heaven. They are ones who have died in a good state. They are heavenly maidens, *houris*. Whether they are boys or girls, they will be in that state. It is a very good death. Do you understand?

AHSIYA: Yes.

IMRAN POSNER (age 6): How do you get to God?

BAWA MUHAIYADDEEN: It is very easy. You have seen dramas and plays, haven't you?

IMRAN: Yes.

BAWA MUHAIYADDEEN: In the practice of Hinduism, people place fruits and incense before the statues of their gods. They light camphor and incense and wave it up and down before those statues. Just as Christians light candles and place them before statues of Jesus ☺, Hindus also practice certain types of ritual worship. They light an oil lamp and wave it in front of their gods. This is not done in order to give light to their god, but to make their own heart a light. They are asking their god, "Make my heart a crown of light." This is their thought. To them the flame they hold before their god is not really fire and should not be seen as such. It should be seen as the person's trust, his devotion, his love, his surrender, and his prayer to God. That surrender, that trust, and that love is what the person is focusing on. Fire is not what should be seen in the heart, but rather a pure heart and good qualities. That is what God sees. So, the one who is holding the flame and worshiping the idol is not really offering fire, he is offering his innermost heart *(qalb)*, and it is his heart that God sees. Similarly, we must offer our heart for God to see.

If you offer your heart like that, you will see God. If you do not look at the world within your heart, if you discard the world and open your heart so you see only God within it, if that love, that trust, and that *īmān* (faith, certitude, and determination) develop within you, then you will reach God. Do you understand?

IMRAN: Yes.

BAWA MUHAIYADDEEN: For example, my son, take a spider. The female spider weaves its web with strands of thread, and upon seeing this, the male is attracted to her and desires her. The female also is attracted to the male. She will dance and then sit and wait for him. He will run here and there and finally go to her. Then the pair will mate, doing what they do in the world. As soon as they are finished, and before her husband can run away, the female catches him and entwines him in the web. Then she kills and eats him. There is no way he can escape. Right after being with that one female, he dies. His wife actually catches him and eats him, and he's finished. That is the work of a spider.

Similarly, the world raises us and gives us food and clothing. But then illusion *(māyā)* comes and entwines us. Four hundred trillion, ten thousand sins and 'spiritual' energies come to capture us, and once they have caught us, they feed upon us and grow, day after day. They suck our blood and weaken our bones, our tissues, and our skin. Our strength and energy diminish. We become weaker and weaker. Finally, just as the female spider consumed its mate, the world and illusion consume us, and when we are all wrinkled, when our nerves and bones are weak and we have lost all our energy and strength, they throw us away. In the end, we will be just like the male spider's corpse that the female discarded—a corpse that can be of no more use.

We have to escape from these sins. The world and the spider are the same. Illusion and that spider are exactly the same. The spider eats its mate. Illusion and bad qualities capture and devour us. All the evil qualities, anger, hastiness, and jealousy will consume us. We have to escape from them. Do you understand?

IMRAN: Yes.

BAWA MUHAIYADDEEN: You must escape from them. Do not end up like the spider.

AHSIYA POSNER (age 7): If you see God, do you see Him with your own eyes?

BAWA MUHAIYADDEEN: You can only see God if you are God, if you become God. My love you. If you want to become an orange, you must become the juice inside. Then you can know its sweetness. If there is no sweetness within it, can you call it an orange? Only if there is juice in the orange will the one who eats it say, "This is an orange. It is so sweet and tasty." Similarly, if you are within God, then the one who is able to understand will understand. The one who can see will see, and he will say, "Oh, this is the juice." Someone who wants to see God has to change into God. He has to become God's qualities. He has to take on God's actions and behavior. He has to become God's words. He has to become God's good thoughts. He has to pursue this ideal and change into God.

When we disappear as a light within God, then we will be like the juice within the orange. We will be able to see the light, the resplendence, and the completeness. It will see itself. It will be like the juice seeing the orange and the orange seeing the juice. Light sees light. God sees God. That is man-God, God-man.

Do you understand? You can see it like that. When you come to that state, you can see it.

ABDUL-RAZZAQ BAUMAN (age 7): How do you destroy satan?

BAWA MUHAIYADDEEN: Satan is afraid of fire. He himself is made of fire, but he is not afraid of his own fire. He is afraid of the real fire. When God created satan and the jinns, He made them out of fire. Satan uses the fire inside himself to burn others and to frighten them. But the fire satan is afraid of is the fire of truth. He is afraid of the fire of God's light and truth. So, when you attain the fire of wisdom, the fire of truth, and the fire of faith in God, then God's good qualities will appear within you. And when the power of that fire is within you, you can destroy satan. You can burn him and chase him away, because he is afraid of that. When the truth dawns inside you and when you speak the truth, satan is afraid. When you have the look of truth and when you act with the actions of truth, satan runs away in fear. Do you understand?

Anything else?

JACOB HURWITZ (age 5): How did God destroy satan? Can God destroy satan with only the fire of His part or the fire of satan's part?

BAWA MUHAIYADDEEN: It is with satan's fire that satan destroys and causes fear. Satan's fire is falsehood. God's fire is truth. It will burn everything evil. Do you understand? God is truth, and everything else is afraid of that truth. When truth comes, satan leaves. He is burned up.

KABIR GREEN (age 5): I have a question. What happens to satan when he gets destroyed?

BAWA MUHAIYADDEEN: A dog eats feces because that is what it likes. It likes the taste of excrement. What does the dog experience when it eats feces? It loves the taste. It enjoys eating feces. In the same way, satan enjoys his work. All evil is tasty to him.

When satan is destroyed, he becomes subject to all the tortures of hell. His house is hell, and the torture he receives there lasts forever. If you yourself escape from that, then that is enough. That alone is enough. You have to find a way to escape. Do you understand?

KABIR: Yes.

ILMI MUHAIYADDEEN (age 6): What happens when you die?

BAWA MUHAIYADDEEN: What happens after we die depends upon the good and the bad we did while we were here. For whatever sins we committed here, we will receive the correct punishment and torture. If we did good things, the angels and celestial beings will come for us and carry us away in golden palanquins.[1] If we did evil, then after we die, the angels that give the punishment in hell and demons with big teeth and horns will come for us. They will beat us and bind us, burn us with fire, and then drag us away. The outcome is according to what we have done while we were here. What we do here is what we will receive there. We have to live our lives always ready to do what is good.

KABEERA MCCORKLE (age 3): How do you get to hell or heaven?

TRANSLATOR: Imran knows the answer.

BAWA MUHAIYADDEEN: Give the answer.

IMRAN POSNER: When it is Judgment Day.

TRANSLATOR: Ahsiya knows the answer.

AHSIYA POSNER: God takes you to heaven.

BAWA MUHAIYADDEEN: Imran said that on Judgment Day you are questioned, and then according to the judgment, you are taken to either hell or heaven. Ahsiya said that if we do good, then we are taken to heaven, and if we do bad, then we go to hell. That is what happens after the judgment. That is what they said. Do you understand?

KABEERA: Yes.

BAWA MUHAIYADDEEN: So those two children have answered you. Anybody else?

---

1. palanquin: A small carriage suspended on two poles which rest on two men's shoulders. Used in some countries to carry people about.

KABIR GREEN (age 5): Does satan take you to hell?

BAWA MUHAIYADDEEN: Yes. That is where he lives. Anyone who has bad qualities lives in hell, and satan will be there. If someone has good qualities, God and heaven will be there. If you make the good qualities grow inside you, then you too will be in heaven. What time is it?

CHILD: Ten twenty-five.

BAWA MUHAIYADDEEN: We did not have time to speak with any of the adults. But that is all right. Precious children, jeweled lights of my eyes, in our lives, on the inside and the outside, we have given birth to hundreds of thousands of children. Without our minds even being aware of it, our mind hatches thoughts the way a fish hatches its young. Each thought of ours is an egg. Just as a fish lays millions of eggs, our mind lays millions of eggs: attachments to the world, evils, all our ideas and intentions, and so many other thoughts created by our attachments. They hatch, and just like baby fish swim and play in the ocean, these thoughts play about and wander around in the mind, which is the ocean of illusion. In the ocean, the bigger fish eat the smaller fish. One fish catches and eats the next. Similarly, in life, when one group becomes larger than another group, it captures and consumes the smaller group. When one race becomes the majority, it consumes the minority.

In life's ocean of illusion, the mind hatches so many baby fish from its changing thoughts. Consider the Arabic letter *mīm*.[2] Man is created from the *mīm*. Then man's mind hatches torpor and illusion, and these in turn catch and eat one another. Because of all this catching and eating, mankind is being destroyed, and this will continue until the whole world is destroyed. Hell is growing larger and heaven is shrinking. Goodness is growing smaller and evil is

---

2. *mīm* (A) This Arabic letter (م) corresponds to the English consonant 'm' and is shaped like a sperm cell. From this comes the *nuqtah*, or dot, which is the form of the world. Here Bawa Muhaiyaddeen is punning on the word *mīm*, which sounds like *meen* (fish) in Tamil.

growing larger. Millions of baby fish are being hatched by the mind. Because of differences of race, religion, and sects and because of attachments to relatives, friends, possessions, and other things, those who are bigger are trying to destroy those who are smaller. The rich are trying to destroy the poor. Each person catches and devours the next. Man is hatching these thoughts in the huge ocean of illusion that is his mind. By feeding such thoughts, he reaches a state where he commits murder and sin. He designates these thoughts to various races, religions, philosophies, and scriptures, and then he ranks them as high or low. But if we look at this state closely and carefully, we can see that just as fish in the ocean catch and eat each other, so human beings, having multiplied in kith and kin, catch and devour one another without knowing who is who. Without knowing who man is and who God is, without understanding that we are all one family, all one group with one God, one person just catches and eats the next. Without understanding each other, one group captures, crushes, kills, and devours another group. This is how those who live in the ocean of illusion act. Man must realize this.

We need to understand our lives. We need to use our wisdom. We need to understand who we are and who our Father is. We must imbibe His qualities of peace and act accordingly. We have to embrace a life of peace. Instead of exhibiting the fire of sin in our hearts and our thoughts, we must show God's quality of peace and speak words of honey. We must show His equality and justice in our actions. Then the kingdom of God will be ours, and we will be able to show others the path by which to attain peace.

We must reflect on this, and each child must be attentive to this goal. If we conduct our life and analyze it carefully, then any child, any person, can know peace. We can all attain tranquillity and live a life of peace. We can reach that house of peace and arrive at the kingdom of God's compassion. We can destroy sin and hell and attain the station of God with all His blessings. We can attain the peace and serenity that is His kingdom and know peace of mind. Each child must strive very hard to do this. Not only do we have to try hard, but all our words, actions, and behaviors must be correct. Each child has to come forward to attain this peace and this peace of mind. This is the triumph of all triumphs, the victory that the children of God must achieve. This state will establish peace for us. Let us trust in this. Let us work hard for this. Let all of us come forward together in unity. *Āmīn. Āmīn. As-salāmu 'alaikum wa rahmatullāhi wa barakātuhu kulluhu.* May it be so. May the peace and blessings of God be upon you all.

November 17, 1984

Session 11

Listen my children.
91

Is it good to give *salāms* (greetings of peace)
to people in passing?
95

How did satan create demons?
95

How does God create angels?
100

If God is One, how could He be in everyone's heart?
100

How was God made?
101

Session 11

A'ūdhu billāhi minash-shaitānir-rajīm. I seek refuge in God from the evils of satan, the rejected one. *Bismillāhir-Rahmānir-Rahīm.* In the name of God, the Most Merciful, Most Compassionate. May all praise and praising be to *Allāhu ta'ālā Nāyan* (Almighty God), the One of limitless grace, incomparable love, and the undiminishing wealth of grace.

My sisters, brothers, sons, daughters, grandsons, and granddaughters, my love you. May God, who has the power to sustain us, protect us all. May the One who has that power look after us, comfort us, and give us His grace. *Āmīn.*

Precious jeweled lights of my eyes, life is a very subtle thing. There is no difference between the life or soul of a small person and a big person. The soul of a young child is the same as the soul of an adult. For example, depending on the type of wire inside a light bulb, it may have five hundred watts, a thousand watts, twenty-five watts, or forty watts. Similarly, a person's body may be either large or small, but the soul is the same for both older and younger people. So, we cannot say that wisdom belongs only to adults or only to children. A big rip can be sewn up with a small needle.

What really matters in our life is how carefully and how subtly we absorb things with our wisdom. Just as we give food to the body to make it grow, we need to give food to wisdom for it to grow. We have to learn all the subtleties, and we also have to make an effort. For our wisdom to grow, we must go through many difficulties. Suppose we plant a fruit tree. If we want to eat the fruit, we have to undergo the difficulties of looking after that tree so it will grow properly. First it must grow and then it must flower. Next, the fruit has to ripen. Only after that can we pick the fruit and eat it. Only then can it give us its taste. But we have to be very careful and work hard to take care of that tree. If we don't, we will not receive any benefit from it.

Similar to this, our body has been formed from a tiny drop, a tiny *mīm* (م),[1] an atom. Within that atom is the whole world—hell, truth, falsehood, good, and evil. So many aspects exist within that tiny atom. In our lives we must work very hard and carefully if we want to reach the shore of understanding all this. We have to find out which things are exalted, which things will benefit us later on. Then we must plant those very things and work diligently. We must plant wisdom, and we must strive with love and awareness. Only then can we experience the benefits.

If we just plant a tree and fail to water or fertilize it, that tree will not benefit us. Only if we tend it with care can we enjoy its fruits. Like that, we have to take good care of our life in order to reap its benefits and its goodness. To reach God we have to strive very hard. We must work hard to do good to all and to help others. We must have good thoughts, do our duty, and be of benefit to all lives. To do this, we have to try very hard and work very hard. We must plant a beneficial crop of wisdom and good qualities in our lives. We must plant each of God's qualities and His ninety-nine powers, His *wilāyāt,* within us and strive hard to make them grow and bear fruit. Only then will we reap the benefits of this life.

(*Bawa Muhaiyaddeen pauses to speak to one of the children:* Hi! You must listen to what is being said here. If you are just going to play, why should we bother to sit here and talk? My love you, my little boy.)

Our goal in life is to be able to receive the greatest benefit possible. But first we must plant, tend, and look after the tree. Life is very subtle. Among all of God's creations, we are the ones who are human beings, and, as human beings, we must acquire a certain wealth—the wealth of grace, the wealth of wisdom, or *gnānam,* the wealth of the soul, the wealth of love, and the wealth of God's compassion. We must also work hard and acquire good qualities. We must plant God's ninety-nine attributes within our hearts and tend that crop, so it will grow within us. Only then can we receive the greatest benefit and the greatest wealth. My love you, my granddaughters and

---

[1]. *mīm* (A) The Arabic letter (م) that corresponds to the English consonant 'm'. In the transformed man of wisdom, *mīm* represents Muhammad ☉. The shape of *mīm* is like that of a sperm cell, and from this comes the *nuqtah,* or dot, which is the form of the world.

grandsons. Please think about this.

Your subtle wisdom is what can sew up the rips in your life. Whatever bad things come to you, it is your subtle wisdom and good qualities that can mend them. But first you have to discover that subtle thing which will help you.

When we look at the world, it seems very beautiful, and we admire it. Whatever our eyes see, they find very beautiful and a wonder to enjoy. Then the mind brings that beauty to us and holds onto that memory and smiles. The teeth smile and laugh. The body enjoys it. In this state, the mind looks at the world and keeps a memory of what it sees. But whenever it looks at the world, it sees the same things, the same glitters. They come and go, over and over again. It is an endless story. The eyes look at this story, and the mind stores these endless memories and then yearns for them. The same things come and go, die and are reborn. They go round and round. There is no relief from them. We have to think about this.

When a beautiful flower blooms, it remains beautiful for a short time. If we pluck it, then it lasts for even less time. We smell it, enjoy it, and after a while it dies. When the flower is on the tree, first it emits its fragrance and then displays its beauty. That beauty calls out, "Come!" On the tree the flower only lasts for a short time and then dies. If a man plucks it, it barely lasts at all. If the mind goes and grabs it, it crushes it right away.

What does a flower do? It shows us its beauty and gives us its fragrance. Everything we see beckons us in this way. Everything fascinates and entices us and grabs us, and then, very quickly crushes us. Just as a flower is crushed if you grab it, the illusions of the world grab us and crush our good thoughts and our good state. What happens after that? We meet with difficulties. As soon as good thoughts leave us, evil thoughts come and then we suffer.

In life, whatever we see looks beautiful at first, but we must not think of it as beautiful. It is like the glue on flypaper. The flies are attracted to the shiny look on the flypaper and go to it, but the moment they sit on it, they get stuck. Like this, the whole world is covered with glue. When we see something and go to take it, we get stuck to it. Then we cannot free ourselves from it. Day after day, it entices us. Time after time, it attracts us. But eventually, it totally destroys us. We must reflect upon this.

What is beautiful to the eye will be dangerous to wisdom. If wisdom looks and analyzes, it will say, "Oh, this is not good." So, we must study wisdom. Why did we come here? We came to learn wisdom and to develop good qualities. This is of the utmost importance. We must study the value of good thoughts, good qualities, and wisdom and use them to acquire God's wealth and His kingdom. We came here to learn that lesson. We have not come to analyze the world, but to analyze and extract what is good from within it. We have not come to analyze man, but to find out what is good and beneficial within him.

When we listen to music, what do we listen for? We listen for the sweetness and we appreciate it and say, "Oh, what a lovely melody." Likewise, what do we look for in food? For its taste. What do we look for in the world? With our eyes we look at its wonders. Each of us is looking for different things. But we have to find out what is within us. What is this world within us doing? What is the hell within us doing? What are the qualities within us doing? We have to first examine these things and then learn our lessons in order to free ourselves from them. Only if we study in this way can we be successful in life. Not only will we find success in our lives, but we will be able to protect and help others. We will be princes and princesses to God. We will be brothers and sisters to all beings and serve them.

Like this, every child, you must clearly know what you have to do. You must look at each situation and act with goodness. This is very difficult to do. You have to work very hard at it.

You may think something is beautiful and touch it. For example, the body of a snake is beautiful, but it has poison in its mouth. Something that exhibits beauty will also give poison. If you grab beauty, you will experience some kind of danger soon after that. Danger is always lurking on paths that we tread unknowingly. Therefore, you have to think. You need to understand life and try hard to find clarity. You must listen to your parents and obey them. To progress, you must analyze truth and learn good qualities and practice them.

Not only must you do your school studies, with clarity you must find within them what relates to the study of your life. You must also study God's teachings. You must honor and show reverence to

God, bow down at His divine feet, pray to Him, and begin to know Him. Precious jeweled lights of my eyes, you must learn to do this. This will be your real victory.

Did you understand what we were saying to you? Now we have to understand what all of you are saying to us. Please tell us what you are thinking about. If you have any doubts or any questions about anything, tell us. If there is anything you don't understand or if you have any doubts you want to clear up, please ask us.

JACOB HURWITZ (age 7): If you are going along, you might want to say, *"As-salāmu 'alaikum"* to somebody, and the other person might want to say back, *"'Alaikumus-salām."*

BAWA MUHAIYADDEEN: *Wa 'alaikumus-salām.* I am a pure human being. I am Islam. Purity is Islam. I am indeed a pure human being. *As-salāmu 'alaikum.*

JACOB: *Wa 'alaikumus-salām.*

BAWA MUHAIYADDEEN: This means: I am a child of Adam ☮, as you are. I am also God's creation. You and I are the same. *As-salāmu 'alaikum.* We are both showering affection upon each other. We greet each other, feel delight, and look at each other's faces with love. We say this greeting to express joy at seeing another person. *"As-salāmu 'alaikum."* With love you embrace him, realizing that you and he are the same. When you reply, *"Wa 'alaikumus-salām,"* it means, "I am also like you. We are all children of the same parents. We are brothers and sisters of the same parents." You say this and embrace each other with love. That is the meaning of this greeting.

May God give us His grace so we can be like this, so we can be one family, without any separation.

Anything else?

JOEL AIGNER (age 8): How did satan create demons?

BAWA MUHAIYADDEEN: That is a very big question. There is no answer to that question. My grandson, God created four hundred trillion, ten thousand beings. He created ants and flies. He created the 840,000 different kinds of beings, such as human beings, donkeys, monkeys, and horses. Each one of these has different qualities. God also created the angels *(malaks)*, archangels *(malā'ikat)*, divinely wise beings *(qutbs)*, illumined beings *(olis)*, saints *(auliyā')*, jinns, and fairies.

When God created the jinns in heaven, He made Abū their leader. After some time, *Allāhu ta'ālā Nāyan* (Almighty God) wanted to create Adam ☮. He called forth all His lights and showed them His resplendent light. Then He asked, "Who will accept this light? Who will accept this resplendence?" The light God showed them was so resplendent that it swallowed up the brightness of all the other lights. This resplendence was brighter than all of them.

When the lights realized that this great resplendence had absorbed their lights, they thought, "How can we accept such a light? It has absorbed our light." So they said to God, "We cannot accept this light. Its resplendence has swallowed all our lights. Since this light is Your power, Your *qudrat*, we cannot overpower it. You have to keep it."

As the others said this, the earth suddenly rose up and said, "I will accept this resplendence."

After acknowledging the first decision, God turned to earth and said, "O earth, you have sought your own destruction. This resplendence is perfectly pure. It contains no blemishes or faults. But you, earth, have so many faults, and yet you are agreeing to accept this pure light. If you do, you must return it to Me in the same condition it is in when you receive it. You can keep the profits you receive from it, but you have to return the capital to Me. Without really understanding this mystery, you have made this choice and thus brought ruin upon yourself." But God said, "All right, I will grant this to you."

Then this resplendence was sent to make the earth, the fire, the water, the air, and the ether each accept and recite the *kalimah*.[2] By doing so, the pride of all five was controlled. Through the power of

---

2. They recited the *kalimah*: *Lā ilāha illallāh, Muhammadur-Rasūlullāh* (There is nothing other than You, O God, and Muhammad is the Messenger of God). For a further explanation of the story of the creation of Adam ☮, see *To Die Before Death: A Sufi Way of Life* by M. R. Bawa Muhaiyaddeen, pages 120–125.

this resplendence called *Nūr Muhammad,* they were made to accept the *kalimah* and accept God as the Almighty One. Before that, each of them had shouted, "I! I! I am great!" But this resplendence proved to them that God was greater than all of them, and thus made them accept Him.

This is a vast story, so I can only tell you parts of it now. Some time after this, God set out to create Adam ☉. He sent down the four angels: Jibrīl or Gabriel, Mīkā'īl or Michael, Isrāfīl or Raphael, and 'Izrā'īl or Yaman (may the peace of God be upon them all) to collect some earth. But by the time the first three angels came, the earth, through reciting the *kalimah,* had attained wisdom and understood the truth, and so it said, "In the name of Allah, do not take earth from me!" So the first three angels returned without any earth. Then God sent the last angel, 'Izrā'īl ☉, to collect earth from all four corners of the world—east, west, north, and south—to gather one fistful of earth. When 'Izrā'īl ☉ went to get the earth (which is Adam), earth said, "In the name of Allah, do not take any earth from me."

'Izrā'īl ☉ answered, "The very One in whose name you are swearing is the very One who sent me to take this earth. If you don't agree, you must speak to Him about it. I must do the work I was sent to do."

Then God spoke to the earth, and after that 'Izrā'īl ☉ took some earth and brought it back to God. He asked, "O God, where can I put this?"

Then God said, "Put it in the place known as *karbalā'.*"[3]

For each human being, *karbalā'* is his own heart, his *qalb.* It is in his own heart that man prays. That is the place of worship, known as *karbalā'.* It is also the *Ka'bah.*[4] And it is also the world, the *dunyā,* where you must fight the battle. All of these are in that one place.

---

3. *karbalā'* (A) The center of the eighteen thousand universes, the battlefield of the heart. Also a city in Iraq, the scene of a famous battle, in which Husain ☉, a grandson of the Prophet Muhammad ☉, was killed.

4. *Ka'bah* (A) The house of God; the most important place of worship, in Islam. In the world it is a cube-like building in the center of the Mosque in Mecca; the place to which Muslims turn to pray. Within the human being, the *Ka'bah* represents the heart, the original source of prayer.

So God told 'Izrā'īl ☉, "Put the fistful of earth in that place." Now, in the world today, there is a place called Jiddah. On the map, it is near Mecca. But that is not the place I am speaking of. Each man has this Jiddah within himself.

Then God said, "O 'Izrā'īl, out of this one fistful of earth I am going to create all lives, and it will be your duty to bring them all back to Me. And in the end, you will also have to bring back your own life."

This fistful of earth was kept in that place for years and years. God made the rain fall on it until it came to exactly the right consistency. This took many, many years. Then God formed Adam ☉ from this earth, and He impressed the resplendent light called the *Nūr* (which He had revealed earlier) onto the forehead of Adam ☉. The spot where that light was impressed is known as the *kursī*, the eye of wisdom. That eye is always there, and when it is open, you can see this world *('ālam)*, the world of the souls *(arwāh)*, and all of everything. So it was on the center of man's forehead that God placed the eye of the *Nūr*. And that is the beauty and radiance of the face of man.

When Adam ☉ was being created out of earth, Abū, the leader of the jinns in heaven, became jealous of Adam ☉. This changed him into satan. He gathered together a thousand fire lives like himself and told them, "Adam is being created. Let's go watch." Satan, with bad thoughts, looked at the form of Adam ☉ and said, "If you remain lower than me and obey me, I will help you in any way I can. But if God creates you higher than me, I will hurt you in every way possible."

When satan looked at the form of Adam ☉, the light on Adam's forehead stared back at him. Then the leader of the jinns said, "You are still only in the form of earth, and yet you dare to look at me so intensely!" This made satan so angry that he spat on Adam's form, and the poison in his spit spread throughout that pure body. At once, God sent the Angel Gabriel ☉ to remove that spit. Gabriel ☉ came, and with two fingers pinched that spot and threw away the spit. That place became the navel, the place of the poisonous umbilical cord. And today, no matter how much we keep cutting away that cord, the evil that already entered the body through it still remains.

Now, after God created Adam ☉, He told everybody to stand

behind him in prayer, but satan protested. "He is only made of earth, while I am made of fire. Why should I stand behind him?"

Then God said, "I did not say that you are to worship Adam. I said that I placed him in front, and you behind. Prayer is only to Me. You will be worshiping Me."

"I know how to worship You, O God," satan replied, "and I will never stand behind Adam to worship You."

"O *mal'ūn,* accursed one who has strayed from the good path, you must worship Me standing behind Adam," God insisted. But satan still refused. Then God scolded him and said, "Because you have strayed from the path, there is no place for you here." And God threw satan out of heaven saying, "Anyone who follows you will not follow Me. And anyone who follows Me will not follow you."

Thus, the commander of the jinns and his one thousand followers were thrown out of heaven. He later became known as satan. What is satan? Satan is actually evil qualities. The four hundred trillion, ten thousand kinds of evil qualities such as anger, taking drugs, arrogance, *karma, māyā,* jealousy, envy, deceit, the qualities of revenge, attacking one another, deceiving one another, and doing black magic against one another are what satan is. There are four hundred trillion, ten thousand 'spiritual' evil forms that are worshiping satan. It is these evil qualities that are called satan.

Now do you understand what satan is? Satan is all these bad qualities. Even if you have one drop of these qualities, that is satan. Whoever has these qualities within becomes satan.

If a snake bites a man in one spot, its poison will spread throughout his body, and he will die. Like that, if a man has one tiny atom of satan's qualities, that quality will spread all over him. Hatred, jealousy, and differences of race, religion, caste, and languages are all qualities of satan. You cannot see satan. He has no form. But you can see his qualities in every man.

Everybody has satanic qualities, except for those who have only the true qualities of God. If you have evil qualities, you are satanic. If you can conquer these evil qualities, you are godly. If you can completely cut away these qualities and acquire God's qualities, then you are man-God. God is within man, and man is within God. God has man within Him and man has God within him. At times when you look at man, he will be like God. At times, when you look at

God, He will be like man. It is this state that we must establish. If we can eliminate the evil qualities, then we can be called a man and God. But, as long as we do not rid ourselves of these qualities, we will be satan. We will have satan's qualities.

You and I must change. Every child must change. We must have good conduct, good behavior, and love. We must acquire and act with these qualities and show kindness to all lives. That will be good. Do you understand now? Did you understand, my daughters, my sons?

ANSWER: Yes.

BAWA MUHAIYADDEEN: You must acquire God's qualities of patience, contentment, trust in God, and giving all praise to God *(sabūr, shakūr, tawakkul,* and *al-hamdu lillāh).* All His qualities shine and resplend. All satan's qualities contain darkness and torpor.

Is there anything else?

IMRAN POSNER (age 6): How does God create angels?

BAWA MUHAIYADDEEN: The same way He created you. You are an angel. Right now you are human, but if you change your qualities, you will become an angel. If you have good thoughts, good qualities, and come to the point of God, you will become an angel.

The angels were created out of fire and light, and the jinns were created out of fire. But you were created out of light. God told the angels that what the heavenly beings do not know, human beings can know. The heavenly beings have thirty-six potentialities, or *tatthwas.* Man has ninety-six. Therefore, if you reach that state of a true human being, you will be even more exalted than they are. Do you understand?

IMRAN: Yes.

AHSIYA POSNER (age 7): If God is One, how could He be in everyone's heart?

BAWA MUHAIYADDEEN: All right. Water flows in the river and all of you drink that water from the river, so you all have that water within you. Isn't that so? There is one river, and all of you drink the same water that comes from it. There is only one sun, but all of you can see it. Understand? There is one moon, but everyone can see that too. If all of these can be seen in this way, how will God be seen? He is within everyone. He is very profound, very deep. My love you.

JAHJE BATH (age 7): How was God made?

BAWA MUHAIYADDEEN: God was within everything that existed naturally. He is the treasure that grew from all of this. He is the essence of all that is natural, the essence of everything all rolled up together. He is a power that grew from the essence of everything and that can control everything.

In the very beginning, there was no sound. Everything was in silence. When He, that power, came out from within all things, a resonance came forth. From that resonance came the explanations. And from those explanations came many meanings, sounds, and understandings. That resonance emerged as the life within all lives. Within these lives, it manifested as feeling, awareness, and intellect. Every being was brought to life. Every seed was brought to life. Everything started to have feeling—but that did not happen until long, long after they were created. That is why it is said, "In the beginningless beginning before the beginning, in *anāthi* before *āthi*, God was in a state of darkness. *Anāthi* was the time of darkness. In that time, God was in a state of darkness, but He came out from that darkness. That is God's achievement and His wonder. This is what He came from. He was not made by anybody. He is the One who made everything. He gave birth to everyone. No one gave birth to Him. But you can reach Him. If you become Him, you can reach Him. If you attain His state, you can see Him. Do you understand?

Okay, shall we stop now? My love you, precious jeweled lights of my eyes. I feel tired now. Shall we stop? Please forgive me. *Al-hamdu lillāh* (All praise belongs to God). *As-salāmu 'alaikum* (May the peace of God be with you).

December 15, 1984

Session 12

Why did God make the planets
if no one lives on them?

Session 12

AHSIYA POSNER (age 8): Why did God make Mars and Jupiter and those other planets if no one lives on them or if there is no use for them?

BAWA MUHAIYADDEEN: Scientists have done research into so many things, and yet they do not know how to do research into their own souls. Even though they have studied for so long, they have not been able to investigate and find a treatment for some of the diseases that are right around them. How can those who have been unable to research into their own souls, know that God did not create anyone on Jupiter? That is not the way it is.

In every place that God created, there are heavenly beings, stars, divinely wise beings *(qutbs)*, saints *(auliyā')*, lights of God *(olis)*, jinns, fairies, angels, celestial beings *(dēvas)*, demons, ghosts, and fiends. There are many beings like these, and they exist in all the places that have been created. You see the stars, don't you? Have you seen shooting stars? Have you seen the stars speak? They do speak. We do not understand their language, but another star will understand. Like this, God has provided what is needed for all His creations. He has not created anything that is useless.

My child, if a fish comes out of the water, it will die. It can live only in the water, so it is there that it must search for and find its food and whatever else it needs. Similarly, we also must have faith. God is within us. Heaven and hell, good and evil, the jinns and fairies, the angels and archangels *(malaks* and *malā'ikat)*, the world and the eighteen thousand universes, everything is within us, but we have not yet discovered them. We have not yet realized what is within us. We have not discovered the heaven in our own lives. If we have not found God, then what is the point of doing research into things like Mars and Jupiter? We should do research within ourselves to discover that treasure, God. If we wander away from that treasure, we will die, just as a fish would die if it left the water. If we leave God and go elsewhere, we will die. We must have the faith, certitude, and determination to do research within ourselves. Only then will we find what we are searching for. Do you understand?

January 5, 1985

Session 13

When you do the same bad thing again and ask for
forgiveness, will God forgive you again?
109

When I hear bad words, I try to get them out of my mind,
but they don't really go out sometimes,
so what should I do?
110

We know that God will always exist forever, but will satan
always exist forever?
110

When Bawa feels better can I sit on his lap?
111

Satan used to be good, so how could he be so bad now?
112

Why did God create satan?
113

Session 13

AHSIYA POSNER (age 8): If you do something bad and you ask God for forgiveness and then God forgives you, and then you do the same bad thing again and ask for forgiveness, will God forgive you?

BAWA MUHAIYADDEEN: God is a forgiving God who will forgive you three times for any fault you commit. After three times, if you commit the same fault again and ask for forgiveness, the fault will be added to your account, atom by atom. After the third time, the fault will be divided into one thousand parts. One thousandth of that fault will be written onto your account. Each time you repeat the same fault, your account continues to increase by one part of a fraction. One by one, these faults will be added on to your account. So, for that one fault, you accumulate fault after fault, and for this there will be a punishment.

Once you have asked for forgiveness, you must try to stop committing that fault. Or, try to stop it the second time you ask for forgiveness. Or, at least, try to stop it the third time. Even after that, through wisdom, you must try to understand what you are doing and try your best to correct yourself. As much as you correct yourself, God will forgive you that much. Asking for forgiveness is good. He will forgive and He will forgive and He will forgive.

Ahsiya, suppose you are wearing a beautiful white dress. If you fall in a place which is full of rust, your dress will get stained, and no matter how much you wash that white dress, the rust stain will still be there. It may get a little lighter when you wash it, but the stain will still be there. If you fall in that rust four times, the white will almost disappear and the stain will be prominent.

The heart is also like this. As long as you keep doing the same things over and over, a stain will accumulate in your heart. The fault will be there. You must understand this. You must try not to let this happen. Asking for forgiveness and being forgiven is like cleaning the rust stain from your dress. No matter how much you may ask for forgiveness, there will still always be a little of that stain there. Do you understand?

AHSIYA: Yes.

BAWA MUHAIYADDEEN: You must not commit that mistake again. Ask for forgiveness and do not do it again. That will be very good. If you do repeat the fault again, then you have to ask for forgiveness again. You will be forgiven, but you really must try not to commit that fault anymore.

KABIRA MIRIAM HOCHBERG (age 7): When I hear bad words, like I hear at school, I try to get them out of my mind, but they don't really go out sometimes, so what should I do?

BAWA MUHAIYADDEEN: Say, *"Astaghfirullāhal-'azīm, astaghfirullāhal-'azīm.* I seek forgiveness from Allah, the Supreme. O God, stop bad words like these from being heard in my ear. And, even if they are heard, don't let them stay in my heart. Take them away." Ask this from God. Then if the memory of those bad words still remains in your heart, you can say, *"Allāhu akbar* (God is great), *Allāhu akbar, Allāhu akbar. Al-hamdu lillāh* (all praise is to God), *al-hamdu lillāh, al-hamdu lillāh."* Say this with your heart. *"Al-hamdu lillāh, al-hamdu lillāh, al-hamdu lillāh."* Then it is these words that will remain in your heart, and the bad words will leave.

Any other questions?

IMRAN POSNER (age 6): We know that God will always exist forever, but will satan always exist forever?

BAWA MUHAIYADDEEN: My grandson, my love you. I have so much love for you. You know what an opposite is, don't you? There is day and there is night. There are good things and there are bad things. Only when bad exists can we know that good exists. If only good existed, we would not know about bad. It is only because there is a hell that we can understand what heaven is. Hell is torture and heaven is peace.

The darkness of the night is fire. That is what satan is. Coolness, love, mercy, and charity are the good qualities of God. That is what God is. Things that can be destroyed have to exist, and things that cannot be destroyed also have to exist. They both must exist, as opposites. When the Final Day, the Day of *Qiyāmah*, comes, many things will be destroyed. What will not be destroyed after *Qiyāmah*? God. God will go on existing.

Therefore, both light and darkness have to exist. One is peace and the other is hell, sorrow. One will perish; the other will not. Like this, satan (which represents bad qualities) has to exist, and good qualities and thoughts also have to exist. These two aspects will continue to exist so that you can understand one by knowing its opposite. But in the end, God alone will remain forever. There also exists a way in which everything will be destroyed on the Day of *Qiyāmah*. Until then, opposites, such as good and bad and heaven and hell, will go on existing. Only if they exist can people who have wisdom find a clearness that will bring them a state of peace. Otherwise, they would never understand the difference between good and bad things. They would not understand anything. They would not be able to learn wisdom.

God knows. God has learned everything, but we have not learned. We are merely creations. Do you understand? It is a good question.

SABURAH AMEENA POSNER (age 4): When Bawa feels better can I sit on his lap? (Everyone in the room begins to laugh and Saburah begins to cry.)

BAWA MUHAIYADDEEN: Good, good, good. My daughter, my granddaughter, when I am well, you must come and sit on my lap. Now I haven't enough strength. Even now you could sit on my lap, but I am not strong enough for it. Later you can come and sit.

The people in the room laughed because they were so happy. Your question made them happy, and that is why they laughed. They were thinking, "We are not as lucky as you. We cannot sit on Bawa's lap!" My love you.

Any other questions?

AHSIYA POSNER (age 8): If satan was so good, how could he have become so bad? Satan used to be good, so how could he be so bad right now?

BAWA MUHAIYADDEEN: Jealousy! Pride and jealousy! He was jealous because God was going to create Adam ☮ in such an exalted manner. He thought, "I was created out of fire. The being who is created out of earth is going to be greater than I am! God wants me to bow down to such a one! How can I do that?" Jealousy, envy, and vengeance crept into him, and those qualities became his vile hell. It is because of those qualities that satan became bad.

Today, or at any time—whenever the qualities of pride, envy, jealousy, vengeance, doubt, and falsehood come into him—a man can become satan. Those are the qualities that make a man satanic. A man who has envy, pride, and anger will always attack others. As a result of this, *karma* and sin envelop and surround him. That is poison. A snake has poison in its fangs because of satan. A human being has poison in his heart because of the qualities of envy, jealousy, pride, and vengeance. A snake bites with its mouth. But human beings bite with their hearts, and that is a deadly poison. Satan became bad because of this, and the man who connects with satan also becomes bad because of this. That is how a good person becomes bad. Do you understand?

We should not take these qualities of satan into us. We should always be humble and have the peaceful qualities of *sabūr* (inner patience), *shakūr* (contentment), *tawakkul* (trust in God), and *al-hamdu lillāh* (giving all praise to God). We should always be humble and have the peaceful qualities of wise men. People who have no wisdom have the qualities of anger, vengeance, envy, and jealousy. No matter how wise a man may be, if he has jealousy, then his wisdom will decrease. Impatience is the enemy of wisdom, hastiness will eat up your wisdom, and anger is the *guru* of sin. No matter how good a man may be, those qualities will always destroy the good thoughts that are within him. You must never allow them to come into you.

You must grow up in this way. And when you grow up and marry and have children, you must tell this to your children. It will give them peace. *Al-hamdu lillāh.*

RAHEEM CONNELLY (age 8): Why did God create satan?

BAWA MUHAIYADDEEN: God did not create anything called satan. God created everything in a beautiful way. He created things that are opposite to each other—things that are good and things that are bad, things with fragrance and things without fragrance. Some people like strong smells, and others do not. There are various kinds of creations. This is the way God has created human beings and other creatures. But some of his creations took the bad things, while some took the good. Those who gathered the bad qualities into themselves changed into satans, and those who gathered the good qualities became saints *(auliyā')*, lights of God *(olis)*, divinely wise beings *(qutbs)*, prophets, angels, and archangels. They changed into good beings and good people. Those who embraced the bad things became bad people, satans. They changed according to what they acquired. This is how people changed into satan.

God never created anything called satan. It was written in *arwāh* (the world of the souls), "Whoever acts against the word of God and has qualities that are opposite to God will become satan. One of the jinns will change into satan." At the time Adam ☮ was created, satan became jealous. He then pointed to God's words and said, "I am that one!"

Has anyone seen satan? In films they may depict him, but no one has actually seen satan. We speak of God, but no one has seen God, either. The Angel Gabriel ☮ brought God's revelations *(wahys)* to the various prophets. We say God's sound can be heard, but we also say that satan's sound can be heard. If we reflect deeply, we will realize that when a man has the qualities of God in him, it is those qualities that will speak to him, and when he has the qualities of satan within him, it is those satanic qualities that will speak to him. When a man has a connection with satan, satan speaks to him, and when he has a connection with God, God speaks to him. So, it is because of their qualities and actions that some people become children of God and others become children of satan. This is how it happens.

If you and I can get rid of the bad qualities within us and fill our hearts with the peaceful qualities of God, then we can become God's children. We have the weapons to do this and to be victorious. We have wisdom, and we also have faith in God. We have God's qualities and actions. With these we can win. We can conquer.

Do you understand Raheem? My love you.

March 15, 1985

Session 14

How do I find God?
117

Session 14

BAWA MUHAIYADDEEN: What do you want?

KABIRA MIRIAM HOCHBERG (age 8): God.

BAWA MUHAIYADDEEN: First, you need wisdom. You have to find that in your heart, it is not on the outside. You need a father of wisdom to give you wisdom. The father of wisdom will give birth to you and raise you within that wisdom. Then you have to give birth to that father. Have that baby within your heart and rock him. If you can raise him within you, then you can see God. If you give your father the milk of love and raise him with that, he will raise you with the milk of wisdom, God's milk. You will have unity in this way. Do you understand? If, instead, you just try to make your face beautiful, it is like a cat washing its face. Cats and dogs lick and clean their faces with their spit. There is no use washing your face with artificial make-up.

March 7, 1986

Session 15

How come God made satan?
121
How come satan is bad?
122
Did God create heaven?
122
If satan was not here, would God be here?
124
Does God tell Bawa what to say, or does he just know?
124

Session 15

CHILD (age 8): How come God made satan?

BAWA MUHAIYADDEEN: Have you seen satan? No, you have not. So, how can you ask why God created satan? You have not seen God, and you have not seen satan. You have heard about them from others. Look into this with your wisdom.

There are two kinds of qualities in man, good and bad. The good qualities are God's qualities. The bad qualities are satan's qualities. If there is light, there will also be darkness. This contrast allows you to understand what the opposites are like. If there is heaven, there will be hell, too. If there is a male, there will be a female.

In the same way, satan is the opposite of God. So, if we have satan's qualities within us, then God's pure qualities will also be there, somewhere over to the side. The evil qualities cannot do anything to God's qualities. They will hover around God's qualities, in the way darkness will be around a light.

At the time Adam ☉ was being created, satan came and spat on that earth form. It was then that he turned into satan. Nothing was created as satan. He was originally Abū, the leader of the jinns in the heavenly world. When Adam ☉ was being created, the evil quality of jealousy got into Abū, and it was that which made him change into satan. He said, "You created Adam out of earth. How can I, who was created out of fire, stand behind one who was created out of mere earth and worship?"

God said, "Do not worship him. Worship Me."

Satan said, "I know already how to worship You, O God. I do not have to stand behind him and worship You." He said many things like that.

Then God said, "O satan, go! *Mal'ūn* (accursed one), you cannot be on this path. Go!"

The bad qualities came to be known as satan. If you can get rid of those qualities, then God's qualities will enter you. When that happens, you will be His fragrance. God is One of perfect beauty. Once you become beautiful, God will be the fragrance. His beautiful qualities contain a sweet fragrance. Evil qualities and actions are foul-smelling. You must transform those evil qualities.

My child, there is no satan, but there are satanic qualities. God did not create anyone called satan. It is we who change ourselves into satan. God created us as perfectly pure souls. So, this is not the fault of God. It is we, ourselves, who created satan. We are the ones who created sin and seek hell. We are also the ones who seek goodness.

Do you understand?

SABURAH AMEENA POSNER (age 5): How come satan is bad?

BAWA MUHAIYADDEEN: Satan became satan because he acquired the qualities of arrogance, *karma*, and *māyā*, and the qualities of the three sons of *māyā* called *tārahan, singhan,* and *sūran,* and so many other evil qualities. If one acquires qualities like these, one becomes satan.

Think about how you cry when you ask for something and do not get it. Then you go and pinch somebody, or you hit someone on the back. What kind of qualities are these? They are wrong qualities. Or think of how impatient you were when somebody else wanted to speak first. It is these qualities that you must get rid of. It is these qualities that are called satan. They are dark qualities. We have seen that satan is darkness. His qualities and actions are dark and black. They are hell. Satan was created out of the fire of hell.

It is we who create satan within us, and it is also we who create God within us. The essence, the power of God, is within us. Satan is the evil nature of hell. That is what takes people to hell. Truth and wisdom will take us to heaven. Both are within us. So, if we change from the qualities of satan and acquire the qualities of God, then satan will not come. Do you understand, Saburah?

JAHJE BATH (age 8): Did God create heaven?

BAWA MUHAIYADDEEN: He created everything. He created you, He created me. Heaven is invisible to your eyes. You have to fashion it in order to see it. Heaven is within you as an atom. If you continue cutting the atom within that atom and look, you will see it. Take one atom of His ninety-nine qualities and cut that one into a hundred thousand parts with your wisdom. Then, take one of those particles and look within it. There you will find ninety-nine, ninety-nine, rotating around without touching one another. If you then take any one of those ninety-nine and cut it into fifty thousand parts and take one particle of that and look, again you will find ninety-nine, ninety-nine, revolving around without touching one another. And if you take one particle from that and cut it into thirty thousand parts and take one particle out of that and look, you will again find ninety-nine, ninety-nine, rotating without touching one another. Then, if you take another part out of that and cut it into twenty thousand parts, again you will find the same thing.

Each time you cut it, the power increases. It is very hard to look at that power. When you do look, you will always see ninety-nine, ninety-nine rotating without one touching the other. Again, take one part, cut it into ten thousand parts and look at that. You will again discover the same thing. Then take one particle of that and cut it into five thousand parts. There, too, it will be the same. And, finally, if you cut one of those particles into one thousand parts, you will continue to find ninety-nine, ninety-nine going around without one touching the other.

It will be extremely hard to look at that power. It will be so bright, so brilliant. It will tear at you and pull you. Those ninety-nine particles will be rotating, without touching each other. When you finally do look at that power, it will completely draw you in. You will fall down unconscious. Such is that power! No matter how long you look at it, you cannot find an end to it. It exists as research within research, research within research. One cannot find an end to the research into God. The ninety-nine, ninety-nine are rotating without one touching another. That is the power of God. He exists as an atom. You must do research into this. Open your heart and do this research with wisdom. When you conduct this research into yourself, you will see the same kind of rotating, without one touching the other. This is something that you must create within yourself. You must bring forth God within you. God created you, and you now have to 'create' God inside you. When 'you' are there, He will not be there, and when He is there, 'you' will not be there. When you and He are there as one, you will be an *'abd,* a slave to Him, and He will be a slave to you.

If you are very rich, you will find that God is even richer than you. If you are a poor person, you will find that God is even poorer than you. If you are learned, you will find that God is more learned. If you humbly say, "I am not learned," He will be even humbler than that. Whatever form you take, He will be higher than you or lower than you. If you are a king, He will be a greater king. If you are a slave, He will be even more of a slave. This is how He exists within you. You must realize this state and create Him within you. When God creates you, He is already within you. He is there within you. He is not to be seen on the outside. He is like the juice within a fruit. Just as we squeeze the fruit and take the juice, we have to squeeze ourselves and take God. Do you understand?

JACOB HURWITZ (age 7): If satan was not here, why is God here? Why would God be useful?

BAWA MUHAIYADDEEN: If there were no darkness, you would not know about light, and if there were no light, you would not know about darkness. These opposites exist in the world. Bad qualities are satan, and good qualities are the qualities of God. If you change the bad qualities in you, then you will never see satan. You will always be seeing Allah. You will always be experiencing peace and tranquillity. Do you understand?

KABIRA MIRIAM HOCHBERG (age 8): When Bawa talks, does God give it to him then, or does he just know?

BAWA MUHAIYADDEEN: The city reservoir is full of water. In that reservoir you may have water that came from rain that fell on that particular day and also water that came from rain that fell earlier. There is also water that came from the river. When you pump water from that reservoir, can you say which particular water is coming out? Can you tell? That is how it is. Whatever comes out, it is coming from the reservoir. Whether it is the water that came earlier or later, we don't know.

May 4, 1986

Session 16

Why did Judas think that Jesus was bad?

Session 16

JACOB HURWITZ (age 7): Why did Judas think that Jesus ☮ was bad?

BAWA MUHAIYADDEEN: Judas did not think that Jesus ☮ was bad. Judas was given some money to buy some things at the market. On the way, he saw a group of people gambling, and he joined them and lost all the money. So he was very worried. He was afraid that if he went back without either the things he was sent to buy or the money, his teacher and the other disciples would be angry with him. Just then, someone approached him and said, "If you point out Jesus to us, we will give you a large sum of money." Judas accepted the offer and pointed out Jesus ☮. He only did this to get some money, that's all.

Today, everyone of us is betraying God. And yet God is the only One who is taking care of us. He is the One who created us and is protecting and nourishing us. But we forsake Him to satisfy all the base desires *(nafs)* of our mind. In this way, we are separating ourselves from God, betraying Him, and allowing Him to be scolded and killed. We are all betraying God. Judas was just one man, but within us are many Judases. If we look at ourselves, we will see them. Every quality in us that lacks truth is a Judas. We have to use our conscience and our justice to look at this.

We hurt so many good people. If they listen to us, we leave them alone, but if they don't listen to us, we destroy them. There are many Judases like this in our minds. We have to think about this.

My grandson, we must not live like Judas. We must change this state and acquire the qualities, actions, and wisdom of God. Only then will there be no place for Judas. As long as we do not have any Judases inside that are trying to ruin and hurt others, there will not be a Judas on the outside.

It is up to us to change. Judas did not come from somewhere

else. Even satan did not come from somewhere else. Both exist within us. Evil qualities are satan. The qualities that are envious, hateful, distrustful, and jealous are the qualities of Judas. These kinds of qualities hurt others and plunder from them. If we can change these qualities, we will have peace. Do you understand?

JACOB: Yes.

May 8, 1986

Session 17

After a person dies and goes to hell,
is it still possible for them to repent and go to heaven?

Session 17

DANIEL ISHMAEL (age 14): *Anbu* (love), Bawa. I wanted to know if after a person dies and they are condemned to hell, would it be possible for them to repent and go to heaven, once they are already in hell?

BAWA MUHAIYADDEEN: After a fruit ripens on a tree, it is plucked. Then someone will squeeze the fruit, drink the juice, and throw the peels away. Do you think that same fruit can be pasted back on the tree and become juicy again? No, it cannot.

In the same way, this cannot be done after death. We must do whatever is beneficial before we die. We must 'die' before death. That is our goal. If we can search for that benefit before our death, then that is what we will be given afterwards. We cannot do this after we die. Once we die, Judgment Day follows. Do you understand?

DANIEL ISHMAEL: Yes.

BAWA MUHAIYADDEEN: Now, while you are here and alive, hasten to work hard to do what is good and try to attain the benefit.

May 25, 1986

Session 18

How do you chase away fear?
137
How come God made people?
137
How do you chase away scary dreams?
138
How can we get our son up for early morning prayer?
139
How did God create the world?
140

Session 18

ISMAIL MICHAEL DIDONA (age 9): How do you chase away fear?

BAWA MUHAIYADDEEN: Fear? If you have the qualities of justice, truth, honesty, wisdom, conscience, God's qualities, and the faith that God exists, then fear will go away because you will have no faults. If you have not done anything wrong, you need have no fear. You will never have fear. Do you understand?

But if you commit faults over and over again, you will be afraid. If you have done something wrong, you will be frightened when you see the police. If you have been playing outside or are in the market when you shouldn't be, then you will be afraid when you see your father or mother, because you are at fault. If you played hooky from school, you will be afraid of your teacher. Fear comes when you have done something wrong. So, if you correct your actions, then you will not have any fear. Do you understand?

ISMAIL: Yes.

CHILD (age 9): How come God made people?

BAWA MUHAIYADDEEN: Why did God make people? Just wait a few years and then see how you will make people! But you have some time yet for that. Your father and mother got together and played, and you came out of that play. They made the form. God merely said, "All right, you have made this form. Now I will make this form rise up and move." If you do not marry, if you do not have a husband, then He will not make people for you. Only if you set out to play will that happen.

In the time before the beginning, called *anāthi* before *āthi*, God created such beautiful souls *(rūhs)*. He created earth life, fire life, water life, air life, ether life, and human life, which is the light life. The lives that arise from the five elements are impure souls. The pure soul is the human soul. It came as light. The impure souls (the lives of earth, fire, water, air, and ether) form the body of man. No creation can exist or have a body without these five elements. But without the soul, there can be no life. That is God's duty and He carries it out. That is what He decreed. This is how you were made. Now let us see what you can create.

God created you. Now let us see if you can create God within you. God created heaven. Why don't you try to create heaven too? God created wisdom. Let us see if you can create wisdom. God created light. Let us see if you can create light. God created sound. Why don't you create sound too? God created truth. You also should create truth. God created the truthful states of justice, compassion, love, honesty, peace, and tranquillity. If you can create these things in the same way He did, then a great, limitless Being, previously unknown to you, will come to life within you.

Instead of asking why God made people, search for the reason why He created everything. Then you will know He created each thing for a reason. Why did He create a flower? He created it because there is a fragrance and a nectar within it. Why did He create a fruit? He created it because it has a taste and gives pleasure and nourishment to people. These are all useful things, are they not?

If you do what is bad, you will go to the wrong side. But, if you stay on the right side and do what is good, you will go in the right direction. If you understand both of these and act accordingly, you will understand why God created or did not create certain things. You have to understand both of these. Do you understand?

JACOB HURWITZ (age 7): How do you chase away scary dreams?

BAWA MUHAIYADDEEN: As long as you keep scary thoughts within you, you cannot chase away scary dreams. The scary thoughts are inside you, always growling and wanting to jump on somebody, or butt them, or beat them up. Because you have these scary things within you, you will have scary dreams. If you can throw away the scary thoughts, then the scary dreams will stop. Do you understand?

JACOB: Yes.

MARGO WEENING, MOTHER OF DHEEN (age 11): We have been trying to get our son up for early morning prayer *(dhikr)*, and he has been going to bed earlier. We haven't been bringing him to break fast at night.[1] But when I wake him up, it takes like twenty minutes to even get him to stir. And this morning I let him go back to sleep. Should I make him get up?

BAWA MUHAIYADDEEN: If you need to make an important journey and you are going to travel in a cart pulled by a horse or bull, if that animal is sleeping, then you must wake it up and hitch it to the cart. If you are not sure whether you should wake up the animal and tie it to the cart or whether you should let it sleep, you will never go on the journey. But if you say, "This is important. I must do it," then you will go on the journey.

Similarly, if you want to train your children on the good path, on the right side, then get them up. This is a very important duty.

MARGO: I shouldn't fear him turning against the whole thing? That is what I fear.

BAWA MUHAIYADDEEN: If you wait and think he might turn against it, he will become spoiled now. Then that much more can go bad later on. "That which does not bend when it is five will not bend when it is sixty."[2] He has to live as a man and grow in wisdom. There is no point in fearing that he will turn to the other side later. He is already turning to that side if you do not make him do it! Get him up with love and patience. Teach him wisdom. Only then will he be your child and will he have love for you and go on the good path. Otherwise, it will be difficult.

If a child tries to drink milk from the backside of a cow, all he will get is urine and dung. So, stop him from doing that. Tell him where the milk really comes from. You must train him in a good way. If you train him for a few days to get up early, then he will

---

1. This question was asked during *Ramadān*, which is the month of fasting for Muslims. The day's fasting ends with the breaking of the fast. Many people come to the Bawa Muhaiyaddeen Fellowship in Philadelphia to partake of this meal.

2. A Tamil proverb.

always get up at the right time.

Look at a little baby who wants milk at three o'clock in the morning. He wakes up automatically when he wants the milk, doesn't he? So, if you teach your son to wake up at a particular time and tell him, "You must get up at three o'clock for prayer," and if you train him regularly, he will get used to it. After that it will work automatically for him.

If you are used to taking a nap after lunch, then the moment you eat, you will feel sleepy because you are used to that. However, if you change your way of thinking and say to yourself that you shouldn't sleep and get used to that practice, then you will stay awake.

Try your best. Try with wisdom and patience, and teach him with love. Then he will learn.

MARGO: Thank you.

CHILD (age 9): How did God create the world?

BAWA MUHAIYADDEEN: Create the world? He created night and day, man *(insān)* and animals *(hayawāns)*. How will you understand this? It is a very great matter. Man suffers all the time, because he is unable to understand the way this world is created. We live in this world for so long without understanding the God who created you and me.

You are asking how God created the world. Look at your state. See how many things you are creating. You create so many things in your mind. Every thought is a creation. It takes on a life of its own. You are the one who gives life to your thoughts, to your mind, and to the things you want, your desires. As soon as you give life to a desire, you then want to act upon it. This is what it means—that you are creating things.

When God created Adam ☻, satan spat his horrible saliva on Adam's body and created evil in him. He is called *sanīsvaran*,[3] because he created evil qualities at the time God created Adam ☻. The name for evil qualities is satan. God created good and bad in order to teach us to throw away the bad qualities and take only what is good.

---

3. *sanīsvaran:* In Tamil, *īsvaran* means god and *sani* means satan.

You came from the world of souls to this place in order to learn. You came to this university of the world to do research into the history of your Father, God, and to know and understand His creations. You need to study and understand your life, who you are, and who God is. You have to come to know everything in every area. To do this, you must study in this university and attain clarity.

Finally, when you discover yourself, your Father, and the wonders of your Father, you will be victorious. But first, you have to study what is within you and discover where your Father is. You must study and know yourself in this university, and then you must know and see your Father who created you. Once you have done this, your examination will be over. Then you will see the Almighty Father. You will go to His kingdom, and you will live in peace in that kingdom of heaven with Him.

God has shown that birth and death exist within a human being. He created these two, birth and death—the world and the hereafter—and put them inside you so you can study them and understand them. Heaven and hell are also inside you. He wants you to study and learn why these things exist. Do you understand?

CHILD: Yes.

May 29, 1986

Session 19

If there were no God, who would create us?

Session 19

MARY FATIMA WEENING (age 4): If there were no God, who would create us?

BAWA MUHAIYADDEEN: Mary Fatima, that is a good question. If there were no God, who would create us? We must know with certainty that the work of creation belongs to God alone. That is the true meaning of creation. If not for Him, there could be no creation. It is God who gives life to the creations. Human beings also create, and so do animals, but only God can give a soul *(rūh)* to the creations and make them move.

Your mother gave birth to you. She made your form, but it is God who made you move. It is God who gives every being the power to move, to speak, to bring forth sounds, to see, and to do other things. What does man create? He creates many, many toys. They may be in the shape of elephants, cats, or mice. He makes dolls. And he also makes idols and statues of gods. But do any of these things speak? No. Can they move on their own? No. No matter how much a person may offer them, can they eat anything? No. Can they walk? Do they go to the toilet? No, they do not.

Man says so many things about the idols he creates, but the idols cannot move or do anything. He creates them and tries to give them powers *(sakthis)* through his own qualities. He tries to give them his speech. He uses mantras, various tricks, or the five letters,[1] because he believes in their powers, and he sends the energies of these mantras to the idols. These *sakthis* are energies that arise from the five elements inside of him. True creation cannot be accomplished by anyone except God. What man creates cannot move.

What does man create? He creates every quality within himself. He creates four hundred trillion, ten thousand 'spiritual' qualities,

---

1. The five letters—*alif, lām, mīm, hā', and dāl*—of the Arabic alphabet combine to form the heart of man.

but every one of these qualities torment him. They are diseases that kill him and lead him to hell. He creates so many things and places his trust in them, but he has no peace. From the day he is born to the day he dies, they give him nothing but suffering. So man creates, but what he creates is his own qualities and thoughts, and he suffers as a result.

All the things that God creates have clarity. They understand good and evil. They also move. Satan creates too, but he only creates evil qualities. Human beings create evil qualities as well as other qualities. But God creates pairs as opposites, so He can show us the differences between good and evil *(khair* and *sharr)*, permissible and forbidden *(halāl* and *harām)*, the sun and the moon, and male and female.

God is the only One who can create and nourish His creations. God is the One who created the whole world *(dunyā)*. He created you, and He is the One who provides your food. He is the One who created the hereafter *(ākhirah)*, and He is the One who summons us back. We must praise Him. If not for Him we would not have been created. No one else could create us. He is the only One we must praise. Mary Fatima, do you understand?

MARY FATIMA: Yes.

BAWA MUHAIYADDEEN: *Al-hamdu lillāh.* All praise belongs to God.

May 30, 1986

Session 20

How do you get over laziness?
149

What would it look like if God did not make anything?
149

Why did we come to this world,
if the world of the soul was so good?
151

Session 20

ISMAIL DIDONA (age 9): How do you get away from laziness?

BAWA MUHAIYADDEEN: Where is the laziness? What is it?

ISMAIL: I don't know.

BAWA MUHAIYADDEEN: Man does not have laziness. There is no such thing. People just call others lazy when they do not make the effort to do their work or their duty. They say, "He is lazy. He hasn't done what he should do. He just sits around or sleeps." When someone doesn't make the effort to do what needs to be done, he is given the nickname 'lazy man'. That's all. So what we need is determination. We need to say to ourselves, "I have to finish this. I need to do this." One who does his duty in this way is a wise person. Do you understand?

ISMAIL: Yes.

BAWA MUHAIYADDEEN: Laziness means not doing our duty, just running here and there and playing. That is not good. We have to do our duty. You and I and everybody must do their duty. Do you understand?

ISMAIL: Yes.

BAWA MUHAIYADDEEN: Say it as if you mean it.

ISMAIL: Yes.

LIZ LEVIN (age 6): What would it look like if God did not make anything?

BAWA MUHAIYADDEEN: Who would see it? You are asking what it would look like? Who would there be to look at it and ask about it? So what is the use in talking about it? There would be nothing to talk about and nothing to ask about. It is only because God did make things that we are all here. Otherwise there would be nothing. There would be no people. There would not even be a person to ask the question that you asked.

God created everything. Now, my child, what you have to ask is, "Where was I before I came here? What other beings are within me? Where have I come to now? After a while, where will I go? Where will I be? They tell me that in the beginning, in *awwal,* I was a soul and that I came to the world then. They say that when I was a soul I did not cry or do anything like that. I was happy at that time. But when I came to the world I saw my mother, my father, and everyone, and I saw everybody fighting. My brother hits me and I hit him. He takes my things and I take his things. We do not have unity. When we look around, we see that everybody is fighting. We just see fighting in the world.

Ask yourself, "How can we live with peace, tranquillity, and unity? How can we find a way to do that? What is the good way and what is the bad way? How can we stop the fighting between brothers and sisters? How can we stop it?

"What I like, my brother does not like. What he likes, I don't like. We even fight about things we both don't like. How can I escape from this? How can I get rid of this sorrow and suffering? How can I find peace?" After you discover the answers to these questions, you have to find out where you will be going from here and what kind of peace you will have there. These are the things we have to understand, study, and know, right now. Do you understand?

LIZ: Yes.

BAWA MUHAIYADDEEN: So study these things. You have to know your own story as well as the story of the One who created you. You have to know what is bad and discard it, and then take what is good and put it to use. Then you must know and understand the greatest, best, most necessary, and most beautiful treasure. Do you understand?

LIZ: Yes.

BAWA MUHAIYADDEEN: It is important to know how God made things and to study the secrets within those things. On a piece of paper, you draw dolls and other things. Why do you draw them? If you did not draw them, the paper would be blank, wouldn't it? Nothing would be seen there. It is only after you draw something that you can say, "This is a doll, and this is another thing." The teacher will then look at it and tell you whether it is good or not so good. It is just like that. Thank you. Right?

LIZ: Yes.

AHSIYA POSNER (age 9): Bawa talked about the world of the soul and how good it was. So why did we come to this world, if the world of the soul was so good?

BAWA MUHAIYADDEEN: This is where the test is. The soul, called the *rūh,* was just a tiny point in the world of the souls. Then it was brought here. It was joined together with the other [the body] to see and understand the many things in the world, to discover what is right and what is wrong, to see what heaven is and what hell is, what truth is and what falsehood is, what patience is and what anger is, what tastes good and what does not taste good, what is beautiful and what is not beautiful. The soul was sent here to study and understand all these things.

The soul is inside of you. There are many other things inside you too. They are in shadow form, but the soul is a light form. There are six kinds of lives. The life sent by God is the pure soul, the light life. The other lives are earth, fire, water, air, and ether. They are the impure souls, and they too are within you. They have life, and the soul has life.

Trees also have life. If you cut a man he bleeds red. If you cut a tree it bleeds white. So a tree has blood, too. Man has red blood. Some kinds of trees also have a reddish kind of blood, a red sap. If you cut them, you can see red blood dripping out of them. Demons live in those kinds of trees. I have seen them. There are many things like this in the world, and we have to understand all of them. There is the sun and the moon. Isn't there a sun and a moon inside of you, too? There are also stars inside of you. Everything is inside you. You came here to understand and study all these things, to know yourself, to know God, and to know the world. You came here to understand all this and then live as a pure soul, to be a light, to join with God, your Father, and to be one with Him—to join as purity with purity, as light with light, as wisdom with wisdom, as grace with grace, as beauty with beauty, as good qualities with good qualities, as justice with justice, and as tranquillity with tranquillity. If you achieve that state, you will see the kingdom of God within you.

We have come here to this school, and the test we must take is to understand and realize all this, here and now. First we have to learn here, and after that we have to go on to the university, where we must learn on the inside. This is why we have come here. God sent us here to study and find clarity. We have to study about the soul, the school, and heaven, the kingdom of God. We have to know about them, understand them, and gain wisdom. That is why we have come to this world.

(The call to prayer can be heard in the background.) *A'ūdhu billāhi minash-shaitānir-rajīm* (I seek refuge in God from the evils of satan, the rejected one). *Bismillāhir-Rahmānir-Rahīm* (In the name of God, the Most Merciful, Most Compassionate). *Allāhu akbar* (God is great). *As-salāmu 'alaikum wa rahmatullāhi wa barakātuhu kulluhu* (May the peace and blessings of God be upon all of you).

Now they are giving the call to prayer. It is time to break the fast.[1] We will get together at another time, when we have to speak and you have to ask. *Al-hamdu lillāh* (All praise is to God). *Sallallāhu 'alaihi wa sallam* (May the blessings and peace of God be upon Prophet Muhammad).

Al-hamdu lillāh. As-salāmu 'alaikum.

June 2, 1986

---

1. This question was asked during *Ramadān*, which is the month of fasting for Muslims. The day's fasting ends with the breaking of the fast. Many people come to the Bawa Muhaiyaddeen Fellowship in Philadelphia to partake of this meal.

Session 21

Is there any benefit in studying Arabic?
155

If someone teases you for not eating meat, what should you do?
157

What prayer should I recite before a test?
159

How does day change into night?
160

Could Bawa comment on children who just sit during early morning prayer but don't recite anything.
160

Every time I want a toy, is that blocking my surrender to God?
163

How do I show my son that the treasures of God are more fulfilling than the things he wants in this world?
164

Session 21

BAWA MUHAIYADDEEN: Does anybody have any questions to ask? The adults can ask too. Big or small, anyone can ask. Any questions? Fatimah, do you have a question to ask? Sitti-Rahman, do you have a question? Joseph? Qadir? What is your name? Ilmi? Daoud?

AHSIYA POSNER (age 9): Is it important to study Arabic? Is there any benefit in studying Arabic?

BAWA MUHAIYADDEEN: There is a great deal of benefit in studying Arabic. Any language that you study can be useful to you. For instance, if you have studied Latin, you may find a job that requires a knowledge of Latin. Or if you know Italian, you may find a job that requires Italian. If you have studied English, then you can use that knowledge in your work. Or if you have studied Hebrew, you can find a job with those who speak Hebrew. Similarly, if you study Arabic, it may help you in life and also on God's path. If you know Tamil, then you can work in places where Tamil is spoken. It is the same with Chinese, English, Russian, or any other language that you study. They can be useful to you in the world. They can help you in life or in finding a job. That is one reason. There are other reasons, too.

If you study the language and learn it with wisdom, if you look within it and delve into it, you will learn about the connection between yourself and God. If you are a person who wants to know how to be devoted, then that is the type of understanding you will gain from the language. If you are seeking a job, then you will understand more about that aspect of the language. If you want to learn to use it for playing a game, then you will understand the game better. It is the same for any language you study, not just Arabic. There is a saying that a learned man is respected in any country.

The Arabic language came last. You can find many explanations within it. All the different aspects of other languages have been contained within the Arabic language. All the explanations given by God to all the prophets have been given in Arabic, in the Qur'an. God's endless secrets, from the time of Adam ☻ right to the end, have been placed within that language. You will be able to understand your secrets and also the secrets of all creations from within the Arabic language. So, it is good to learn Arabic.

If you go on this path with wisdom, if you go beyond scientific knowledge to the station of true knowledge, then you can understand. If your heart is the same as God's heart, if you have perfect purity, then you will receive many explanations of wisdom. If you can study Arabic in that state, you will understand many things. But if you merely study it as a language, it will not help you at all. Whether English, Hebrew, or any language, if you study it merely as a language, it will be of no use to you. But if you study Arabic with the intention to understand what is within it, you will find that it contains all the meanings from all the languages. Everything that you need to study is within it.

Everything is contained within the world. Many secrets are within the earth. The sky also has many secrets. It contains countless lights, stars, and hidden beings such as jinns, fairies, angels, and heavenly beings. And hidden within the earth are worms and insects and beetles. There are seven worlds below. There are so many creatures hidden within the water. In the air there are many organisms we do not see, and in fire there also are many hidden things. There are many beings in earth, fire, water, air, and ether that we will understand only if we study each of those particular sections.

If you want to learn Arabic, you must have the correct approach and learn all the meanings that need to be understood. God has buried everything within that language. That is true wisdom, or *meignānam*. There are different kinds of wisdom: false wisdom *(poignānam)*, ignorance *(agnānam)*, scientific wisdom *(vingnānam)*, and true wisdom *(meignānam)*. You must use true wisdom to do your research. Do you understand? There are many people who, even though they speak Arabic, do not understand all that Arabic has within it. I have not studied Arabic.

Only those with wisdom will understand this. You must understand more. And when your heart, your *qalb*, attains purity, you will understand even more. Your wisdom will be clear, and your heart will be pure. If you have no differences within you, then you will understand still more. Do you understand? *Āmīn* (So be it). It will be good if you make an effort to study and learn the Arabic language.

AHSIYA: I have one more question. In school, if someone says, "You don't eat meat!" and makes fun of you or teases you, what should you do?

BAWA MUHAIYADDEEN: Very good. You can say, "I am a Muslim," or "I am a Jew," or whatever you understand yourself to be. Or you can say, "I am a vegetarian," or "I am a true human being." You can say, "I thought about this with my wisdom, and I realized that my body and the body of animals have the same kind of blood. Whether it is a chicken or a cow or a goat, its flesh is the same as mine. Then I thought, how can I eat that flesh? I also saw that animals have the quality of attacking, killing, and eating others. Vegetables do not do that. So if I eat the flesh of animals, my qualities will become like theirs. I thought about this a great deal, and I decided it was not good for me to eat meat. If I did, I would become an animal too. Even though I was born a human being, my qualities would change, and I would develop arrogance and *karma*. I might even kill others, the way animals do. So I decided that if I gave up eating meat and ate mild things like vegetables, then I would have serenity and peace of mind." This is one thing you can tell them.

There is another thing that you can tell them. Say, "There are many religions in the world. Some of them practice what is called *halāl* and *harām* (what is permitted and what is not permitted by God). This exists in both Islam and in Judaism. The practice of *qurbān*[1] (ritual slaughter) is also found in both Islam and Judaism. Through this practice, meat is made kosher, and then people know what they can eat and what they should not eat. But we see that nowadays people are doing the opposite of this. They disregard the kosher laws and eat all kinds of food indiscriminately.

---

1. *qurbān* (A) The ritual method for the slaughter of animals to purify them and make them permissible *(halāl)* to eat. For a further explanation of *qurbān*, see *Asmā'ul-Husnā: The 99 Beautiful Names of Allah* by M. R. Bawa Muhaiyaddeen, pages 180-184.

"In school these days they even say the name of God must not be mentioned. And if we look at people, they do not seem to be practicing what their religions preach. They say we must eat only kosher food, but the food they eat is not prepared in a kosher way. Now even the people in these religions are eating what they, themselves, said we should not. So, regarding *halāl* and *harām,* they are going against their own word and against the word of God. Therefore, I decided I do not want to eat meat anymore. That is why I gave it up. Rather than preaching one thing and then acting another way, I thought I would give up eating meat, and I would eat vegetables."

Do you understand?

AHSIYA: Some of the kids in my school like my meat, the fake soy meat, better than their meat. At lunch time, sometimes I let them have half of my sandwich if I can't eat the whole thing, and they like my meat better than their meat.

TRANSLATOR: Your meat?

AHSIYA: Fake meat.

BAWA MUHAIYADDEEN: See what happens! They themselves realize it, don't they? So now you can correct them. Tell them that regular meat comes from murdering another life, but this other 'meat' comes from plants. If you eat meat or fish or dried fish, your body smells terrible. Your sweat stinks, and when you go to the bathroom there is a terrible smell. But when you eat this kind of 'meat,' vegetable meat, your body does not smell so bad and even the bathroom does not smell as much.

We ourselves can recognize this. Our own nose will inform us. Tell them that this food is not only more tasty, but it also helps to take away our body odors. Tell them that you have a grandfather who tells you these things and that your mother and father heard this from him and trained you in this way. Say, "Our family too liked eating meat at one time. But little by little, when we gained more understanding, we stopped. Now we eat this fake meat, which is more tasty and less smelly." Do you understand?

AHSIYA: Yes.

BAWA MUHAIYADDEEN: Any other questions?

AHSIYA: In Arabic class our teachers, Naz and Shams, tell us that before we do anything to say the three *Quls* and the *Fātihah*. And on time tests, like sometimes on tests they time you, well I always think of saying my *Bismin*, the three *Quls*, and the *Fātihah*,[2] but it is a timed test and I do not have enough time to or else I will not finish the test. So what should I do then?

TRANSLATOR: Is this a time test set by your Arabic teachers or in school?

AHSIYA: In school.

BAWA MUHAIYADDEEN: That is a very good question. God is a point. You say, "O God, please fulfill my intention. I have faith in You. I trust You." Think this in your heart *(qalb)*. Say, *"Bismillāhir-Rahmānir-Rahīm.* It is from You that I need all my help," and then start writing. That is all you need. Say, *"A'ūdhu billāhi minash-shaitānir-rajīm.* O satan, go away! *Bismillāhir-Rahmānir-Rahīm.* O Allah, I am writing this through You." Then start writing. That is all you need to do.

AHSIYA: So you mean say your prayers at the same time?

TRANSLATOR: No, you don't need to say all the prayers. Just say, *"A'ūdhu billāhi minash-shaitānir-rajīm,"* and then say "O God, You are the One who is writing for me. *Bismillāhir-Rahmānir-Rahīm.* I place all my faith in You." That is the entire prayer, Bawa says.

BAWA MUHAIYADDEEN: Recite the other prayers when you are not taking an exam, when you are at home. But when you do not have enough time, say this short prayer.

When you were a little baby sucking milk from your mother, you had to be held in a certain way. You had to put your mouth on her nipple and start sucking. Then when you started drinking from a bottle, you held the bottle in one hand and sucked on that in a

---

2. *Bismin* (A) A shortened form of *Bismillāhir-Rahmānir-Rahīm:* In the name of God, Most Merciful, Most Compassionate. The three *Quls* refer to the last three *sūrats* (chapters) in the Holy Qur'an: *Sūratul-Ikhlās, Sūratul-Falaq,* and *Sūratun-Nās.* The *Fātihah* is the opening chapter of the Qur'an, the *Sūratul-Fātihah*.

different way. Later, when you started eating by yourself, you ate in still another way.

Like that, what you do depends on the particular situation. You cannot do the same thing in all situations. You have to change according to the circumstances and the surroundings. As you grow older, you will need to use your wisdom and your innermost heart, your *qalb*, to help you decide. You will not be able to recite these prayers in every situation. What you need to do will depend upon the circumstances. Do you understand?

AHSIYA: Yes.

BAWA MUHAIYADDEEN: Say, *"A'ūdhu billāhi minash-shaitānir-rajīm. Bismillāhir-Rahmānir-Rahīm.* Allah, I am asking for Your help," and start writing. That is all you need to do. Anything else?

SITTI-RAHMAN BIBI (age 12): How does day change into night?

BAWA MUHAIYADDEEN: How does day change into night? Day does not change into night. Day is day and night is night. A girl remains a girl and a boy remains a boy. That does not change, does it? There is night for twelve hours and day for twelve hours. In the west there may be more of one and less of the other. There is a time of day and a time of night. The daytime is the work time and the nighttime is the sleep time. Do you understand? Day cannot change into night and night cannot change into day. Do you understand?

SITTI-RAHMAN BIBI: Yes.

BAWA MUHAIYADDEEN: Any other questions?

LOU WILSON, FATHER OF JONAH (age 8): I'm not a little child, but I'd like to ask a question that I think would affect a lot of children. I can't mention any names, but at *dhikr* (early morning prayer),[3] for several weeks now I've been trying to get a certain person to recite

---

3. The early morning *dhikr* refers to the recitations of the names of God and the salutations to the Prophet Muhammad ☮, the prophets, *qutbs,* and angels. This *dhikr* is recited every morning before sunrise in the Mosque of Shaikh M. R. Bawa

the *dhikr,* instead of just sitting there, but this person refuses. And I said, "Why?" And he said, "Because none of the other people do it. None of the other children do it, and I don't want to do it by myself." And the last couple of mornings I have looked around and I saw children sitting at *dhikr,* but they were not saying anything. They were just sitting there. I wonder if Bawa could comment on this?

BAWA MUHAIYADDEEN: That is because those people think they have acquired *gnānam,* or divine wisdom. When a buffalo goes into the river to bathe, what does it do? It stirs up the mud and then rolls around in it. When it comes out of the water, its body is plastered with mud, yet it claims it has completed its bath. Now, that buffalo thinks it is very pure and very clean! And when an elephant, which is a huge animal, goes to bathe, what does it do? After it comes out of the water, it sucks up mud from the river bank and smears it all over its head and body.

Why do these people want to come to the mosque? They can stay at home. Do not look at them. If you come, do your own work and get your reward. Do not join these people. Do your own work. Then you will receive the right reward. Do not worry about those people. According to their wisdom, they have ascended to great heights, but actually, they have fallen into the mud.

LOU: It's one of my children. I feel responsible.

BAWA MUHAIYADDEEN: The way to correct your children is with your own qualities. First, you must correct yourself and your qualities. Then the children will see you and correct themselves. If you are doing something wrong, how can you correct your children? You must correct yourself before you can correct your children. In the same way, in every matter, every one of us must make ourselves clear before we set out to correct others.

It is true, there are some who sit in the mosque without reciting the *dhikr.* If you set out to correct them, that is wrong. They will sit there silently, thinking what they are doing is great, but after a while they will realize they are not progressing. Their farm will not be producing, so they will not find any crops. When they see that

---

Muhaiyaddeen. For the complete recitation see the pamphlet, *Morning Dhikr at the Mosque of Shaikh M. R. Bawa Muhaiyaddeen.*

nothing is growing, they will say, "Oh, this is useless," and they will leave. Since they did not plow the land, fertilize it, or sow anything, how can they expect a crop? They just sat there lazily. That is the lazy group. They expect a rich harvest without working for it, without plowing or tending the land. What is the point of that? Some people may be like that.

But, what is a Sufi like? Each of the 43,242 breaths he takes in a day moves through his body in the same way his life moves through his body, and each breath is bowing in reverence before God. That is work. Just because a Sufi appears silent, it does not mean he is not doing anything. His breath is doing its *dhikr*,[4] which is the connection between him and God. It goes on automatically, "dun, dun, dun." In the same way as the heart continues beating, although we are not aware of it, a Sufi's breath, his *dhikr*, is beating "dun, dun, dun, dun" with the connection to God. That is the *dhikr*. That word goes and beats against Allah with every breath. That is true *dhikr*, where every breath is bowing and prostrating to Him.

But what you are talking about is a very different matter. These people are sitting in the mosque thinking they have attained that state. I sit quietly for a little while sometimes. They see me and think they have reached the same state and that they too can be silent. Well, I taught them the silent *dhikr* at the beginning, but because they were unable to do it in the right way, I went back to the first step and taught them five-times prayer *(tholuhai)*, hoping they could grow through that method.

Never mind them. You try to earn for yourself. The more you work, the more you will reap. That will be of benefit to you. If you try to tell them, they will be angry. Let them realize for themselves and change if they feel like it. If they realize and work hard, they will reap a good harvest. Otherwise, they will just remain silent, thinking their harvest will be the richest. But in the end, they will find nothing. Everyone else will reap something, but they will be empty-handed. The thought that brought them to the mosque and made them sit there at that hour of the day might at least bring them some gain, but it will not bring a rich harvest. The mere fact that

---

4. *dhikr* (A) The remembrance of God, *Lā ilāha illallāhu* (There is nothing other than You, O God. Only You are God).

they woke up in the early hours of the morning and took the time and trouble to come here to sit in the mosque will not be totally in vain. They will gain something, but since they did not work hard, their harvest will not be a rich one.

Suppose you dial a telephone. Unless you say, "Hello" and speak, no one will hear anything. No one will know who is there. So, if you merely hold the telephone up to your ear, what is the use? In the same way, if you go to the *dhikr* and sit there without opening your mouth, it will be like dialing a number and then not speaking into the phone. You will not receive an answer, and no one will hear you. These people think they are highly evolved, so if you try to tell them anything, you are the one who may get hurt.

Try telling them gently. If they listen, that will be good. Otherwise, leave them alone. After all, I have told them so much, so many times. If they have wisdom, they will do it.

My children are good children. If they use their brains, they will escape. All right. Is that all? What else?

DAVID FEDERMAN, FATHER OF JESSE (age 9): A few weeks ago, driving home from the *dhikr* with my son Jesse, Jesse asked me an important question which I have been giving a lot of thought to in the last few weeks, and I would like Bawa to help answer. Jesse said to me, "Dad, if my duty is surrender to God, every time I want a toy" (and our kids today want a lot of toys because they're seeing so many of them on television) "is that blocking my surrender to God?" I think the question for me as a parent is how do I strike a balance between those desires of a child to have toys and to play, but also to do his duty to God and to concentrate and focus on prayer? What kind of balance should we be striking as parents?

BAWA MUHAIYADDEEN: Very good, very good question. It is a good question that your child asked, and it deserves a very good answer.

Look at all the wonders that are around us in the world. Some are right and some are wrong. Show your child what is right and explain that to him. Give him the wisdom, the explanation. That is the section belonging to God. What is on the left side is the section of satan. Do not teach him the things on the left side, the wrong section. What is on the right side, God's section, is limitless beauty, limitless goodness, and limitless joy. There you can find many treasures that are beyond measure: true qualities, true beauty, true wisdom, the true taste, joy, *sabūr, shakūr, tawakkul,* and *al-hamdu lillāh* (patience, contentment, trust in God, and all praise to God). First, you must learn about these. Then, when your child asks you for something, teach him to buy things that belong to the good side. Tell him that the things on the bad side do not belong to us and we should leave them alone. Marijuana, drugs, opium, lies, theft, treachery, deceit, gambling, backbiting, hypocrisy, revenge, intoxicants, lust, theft, murder, falsehood, arrogance, *karma,* and *māyā*— all these bad qualities and actions have to be eliminated. There are many other things that are bad. Do not buy him those. Even if the child likes them and wants them, do not buy those things for him. Give him things that are good. This is your duty. Do you understand?

DAVID: Yes.

BAWA MUHAIYADDEEN: Do it that way.

DAVID: How do I show my son that the treasures of God, the wealth of God are as fulfilling, even much more fulfilling, than the things he wants in this world? You can't lecture, you have to show. How do I show?

BAWA MUHAIYADDEEN: Show him to the extent of your wisdom. If you have wisdom, you can show him. Otherwise, you yourself have to learn. Don't you already know the difference between feces and food? Don't you know the difference between sweet and sour, between a bitter taste and a sour taste, or between light and dark? In this way, understand the differences and then show the child in the same way.

Only if you have wisdom can you show your children. If you have less wisdom than your children, then you are the one who has to learn. If you want to give them explanations, you have to come up to the level of being a teacher, which means that first you have to learn the good things yourself.

Learn what needs to be learned properly. Understand what needs to be understood clearly. Even though we cannot show God, we can show the qualities and actions of God we have acquired within us. Even though we cannot show them a place called hell, through our qualities we can show them the hell we have within us. Heaven can be shown by the peace and tranquillity within us. We have two kinds of vision within our eyes, the good and the bad. Explain these to him. Say, "My son, this is not good. This is good." Do you understand?

DAVID: Yes.

BAWA MUHAIYADDEEN: Explain it in this way.

June 21, 1986

Session 22

In *Maya Veeram,* why do you call it the ABCD world?

Session 22

BAJIR CANNON (age 8): In *Maya Veeram*,[1] why do you call it the ABCD world?

BAWA MUHAIYADDEEN: ABCD is a language that is capable of deceiving the world. It is a kind of speech that makes people lose the four virtuous qualities of modesty, reserve, respect, and fear of wrongdoing. The ABCD world is such that anyone who has studied this ABCD language can deceive anyone he wants, to whatever extent he wants, wherever he may go.

'A' is a section which stands for *ēmāttam*, or deception. 'B' stands for *pee matham*, or fecal arrogance.[2] One dances in accordance with one's arrogance. Fecal arrogance makes you dance to the music of *"Tai, tat, tara, tat,"* without any clothes on your backside. 'C' stands for the Tamil expression of disgust, *"Chee, chee, chee."* When some people see those who have good conduct, they discard them like a dog, saying, *"Chee, chee, chee!* Go away!" And when they see people dressed in only a half a yard of cloth, they open their mouths and say, "Ah, ah, ah!" and welcome them. Instead of wearing a *sārī*,[3] which is six yards long, some women wear clothes made of only a quarter yard of material. But if you look at this with wisdom, you will be disgusted and say, *"Chee, chee, chee!* What is this!" Finally, 'D' is the sound of attacking others, the sound of *"Idi, adi."*[4] Wherever you go, people are fighting, hitting, beating each other, and boxing. They are attacking or killing this one and that one. Some people need to fight and punch and murder. This is how it is in the ABCD world.

---

1. *Maya Veeram* is a book by M. R. Bawa Muhaiyaddeen.

2. *Ēmāttam* is pronounced *aymāttam*, and in Tamil, the letters 'p' and 'b' are written the same way.

3. *sārī* (T) In some parts of the world, instead of wearing dresses, women wrap long lengths of cloth around themselves called *sārīs*.

4. *idi* and *adi* are Tamil words which mean to strike, beat, or hit.

Maya Veeram means the strength of illusion. The section of illusion is the ABCD world. See how many people have been ruined by it! However, if you do not study the ways of this ABCD, you will have to fall into a well.[5] You will be unable to take care of your life, and you will ask, "Where am I going to die?" People will reply, "Go fall into a well or a pond or a ditch, and die." You will have no place to earn a living.

That is how it is. Study this and see. My grandson, learn about this and then see how many tricksters there are in the world and how few men of true wisdom are to be found.

Vandi Pulahan, Kandi Pulahan, and Sandi Pulahan do exist.[6] Look at them. This world is their kingdom. Know-it-all Fool, Unwitting Fool, Plain Fool, and Blind Fool also exist.[7] These four fools have joined together and are running the governments. Only fools will run the governments. All the intelligent people will stand aside. Four fools have joined together to govern the nations: a fool who is learned, a fool who is not learned, a fool who has clarity, and a fool who lacks clarity. That is the kingdom called the world. That is what the book, *Maya Veeram*, says.

Wherever you look, you will find that all are fools. The kings are all gone. When there were kings, there was justice. As soon as the commoners took over, everything went wrong. Kings have become beggars, and beggars have become kings. Those who were high have become low, and those who were low have become high.

So, my grandson, do you understand?

BAJIR: Yes.

BAWA MUHAIYADDEEN: Study the ABCD, but while studying it, push away all the tricks that come along with it. Pick up only what has clarity. Retain whatever has clarity, and discard the tricks.

October 18, 1986

---

5. See *Maya Veeram*. The four fools fall into a well and need to be rescued. Chapter 7, pages 117–129.

6. Deceptive characters in *Maya Veeram*.

7. See *Maya Veeram*, Chapter 7, pages 117–129.

Reflections

When I was little, I remember clearly sitting at the edge of Bawa's bed and listening in wonder as he spoke wisdom that I knew I'd need when I was older. When, at the end of a discourse, Bawa would ask for questions, I remember wanting to know and question all, the universe, and the cosmos…but having only the vocabulary of a six year old I generally sat silently. Now, twelve years later I realize how privileged I was, in having had the opportunity to sit there when he spoke. And when a question arises that I wish I would have asked, I know I can look to Bawa's books, and there, find the answers to anything.

Rahman Beckwith, age 21

I saw God's light in Bawa's eyes. He had so much love in his eyes. When I entered his room, I felt his light. I felt happy and I felt that Bawa was a great saint. How I appreciated what he was doing. It made me tranquil. I was very happy when I went to Sri Lanka to visit Bawa. Bawa was a very exalted being. When I looked at Bawa, he drew his light into my heart. He embraced me with all the love. It was so blissful. When I look at the past, I realize what a great wonder it was for me in my life to meet Bawa. When I went to his room, I felt his peace.

Harry Beltrani, age 27

In the name of God, the most merciful, the most compassionate. There are so many things that the children and grandchildren of Bawa Muhaiyaddeen can learn—can continue to gain—from his teaching. Because of the sheer volume of lessons that come from being raised under the wing of an enlightened saint, I will pick one that becomes increasingly valuable as I become more exposed to the world.

Within every human being is a source of understanding. Even though that source goes by many names, it remains the same. What Bawa has told us many times, has constantly reminded us, is that each and every human being has the ability to find that source within themselves. The source of wisdom is there at all times, we carry this weightless treasure with us everywhere. The more we listen to this voice, the true voice of the Sufi Sheik, the stronger it can become. Only when those teachings that were given through the body of our sheik resonate with that inner sheik will we gain any understanding. This real teaching can help us learn, and help us to correct what is not right in our lives. No religion, cult or philosophy will be able to take us to that place. Only by listening to the voice of conscience, which is directed by wisdom, *which is within,* is it possible to attain this birthright.

All the billions of humans on this earth have the potential to attain the highest state. We are blessed only because we have a teacher to remind us of this. It can be a frightening thing to have such a responsibility. It may be easier to say to oneself, "I could never possibly attain such a state as the Insan-Kamil, the enlightened human being." This is wrong. Bawa is the living example that we have been blessed with, so that we *can* attain that state. He is the example of the Insan Kamil, one in the state of man-God, God-man. He came here to show us how to act, to remind us, so that we too may have that wisdom. Remembering this birthright, the ability to find that pure and spotless purity within ourselves, is not an easy thing to handle. It must be protected like a precious jewel. Although it is far easier to deny that we have that blessing so that we can behave as our mind and desire dictate, it is too late: the secret is out!

Ilmi Muhaiyaddeen Elijah Granoff, age 24

As a young girl, growing up a child of the Fellowship community, I was embarrassed a lot. I was embarrassed of my non-western name; I was embarrassed of taking Arabic classes instead of ballet and of eating Fripats instead of hamburgers; I was embarrassed that my mother wore a scarf when she came to pick me up from school, etc., etc., etc. But, never ever ever do I remember being embarrassed of Bawa; *no shame could ever have been derived from being his grandchild.*

Although to have a guru, to have a sheik, was not "normal" (which is an issue of grand importance to a nine-year-old), it did not matter. I *liked* that it wasn't normal, or, rather, it never occurred to me that it was abnormal, because that word had a negative connotation for me at the time, and Bawa could never have been negative, he just *was*. Bawa was mine and only mine when I went out into my grade school world, no one else knew him, but this "abnormality" was no source of embarrassment; it was a source of **pride**. Because Bawa was pure goodness and kindness and love, and *he was my grandfather.*

Those sources of embarrassment that I ran into as a child were of the world; they were on a shallow level that a nine-year-old cannot perceive as being shallow. But, even to my nine-year-old logic, I could see, *I inherently knew,* that Bawa was on a much much higher level, where embarrassment could not dwell. In its place live my memories, which bring a smile to my face and warmth to my heart every time I think of them. I remember discourses that I did not understand, but which provoked amazing images in my young mind. I remember chocolate kisses, and his medicinal meals and words, and his hugs, and his smile, and a connection that traversed language barriers. I remember my nickname "Birds" and kindness and light and love. **Pure love.**

Bawa taught me what true respect is. He taught me what kindness and love are, and what being a good human being is all about. Now that I have grown up a little and appreciate having an interesting name that means something, and am so thankful that I was not raised eating meat, and the Fellowship is no longer a source of embarrassment, I see that Bawa also taught me how to learn lessons, and what growing up is, and what it is to *appreciate*. Bawa taught me, *he taught everyone,* how to be a good person and still live in this world. He taught me to replace embarrassment with gratitude. And that is the feeling that I am left with when I think of Bawa and the Fellowship; no embarrassment, but gratitude. And, of course, love. **Pure Love.**

Kabira Miriam Hochberg, age 24

I remember the sounds of chirping birds, and wind whispering through leaves of trees right outside Bawa's window. I remember the rhythmic hum of cars, passing every now and then on Overbrook Avenue. I remember that soft, familiar chime his clock made as each hour passed. I remember the tocking murmur of a loosely-fixed fan that circled above me when I sat in his room—gentle breeze across my back. I remember squishing into the tiniest space still left in his room as he began a discourse and all of his children sat around his bed, shoulder to shoulder. I remember hugging his frail body, my soft child's cheek against his smooth, wrinkle-free skin ... and that funny, fuzzy feeling that his white beard would leave lingering on my face. I remember his thin, outstretched palms, filled with candy *just for me*. (Well, not really. He gave sweets to *all* of his children *all* of the time—but, somehow, I felt that he always gave *me* more. He *did* always call me his "sugar box," knowing of my sweet tooth.) I remember his eyes—those brown pools of light, deeply intent at times, lightly smiling at other times—and that wonderful grin that would spread across his face, completely contagious.

But these are just the easy parts to convey of my memories of being with Bawa—for they are tangible sights, smells, tastes, and sounds that were a part of my time with my "grandfather" ... and so, they are a part of me.

Then, there is the whole other realm. Removed from the time, space, or physicality of being with Bawa in his room. It is the realm that transcends the senses—and so, it is a realm that can still be visited even though Bawa's physical form is no longer here. I remember the feeling that being in Bawa's room would bring to me ... deep inside my chest, touching my spirit. It was a feeling of complete peace, of total safety, and of the most deep, unconditional love I have ever experienced. As I sat there, before my Bawa, it was as if nothing else existed but that loving calm that permeated the room. All else was forgotten.

And I sat very still, staring up. I sat, *not* fearful or even in awe of this wise sufi who sat before me; I just sat with the simple knowledge that everything was all right because I was exactly where I belonged. And "where I belonged" did not mean a physical location at all; it meant that state of being and heart-ful feeling that entered my soul each time I was in his presence.

The cozy warmth inside the room rose with everyone's bodies huddled next to one another. And, it rose in sync with the most pure love that could be resonating from a heart. A love that overcame my small being, a love that cushioned me in its warm embrace. It was a love that flowed freely through Bawa's eyes, his smile, his every word ... a love so real, that you could almost *see it* connecting you to him. And, all at once, it was as if time had stopped, and a new space had been entered into. A space in which the *complexity* of 'Truth' had somehow been *simplified* to just mean that very love and goodness and safety and peace that all of us were feeling just by being in Bawa's presence.

Yes, it was that simple.

Today, no doubt, that simplicity is often lost as life becomes increasingly fast-paced and hectic, often delivering us harder and harder blows. Of course, this then makes it hard for me to re-visit and truly enter that soft and simple realm. It makes it harder to return to that feeling that had nestled deep within me each time I sat, squished, in his room.

But, when I can quiet my mind, calm my breathing, and close my eyes for even just a moment ... there's an image that visits me. It is the image of my Bawa's face on one afternoon when I sat with him in his room, shortly before his death. On that day, he turned to me and kept repeating my name, "Ahsiyama, Ahsiyama,"* bending towards me, hand-to-heart. He smiled down on me with the most love welled up in his eyes and his face that one might ever imagine. That ultimate smile to melt the heart and dissolve all worries and anxieties. And he just kept smiling at me with those eyes and that love.

And so, he smiles still.

Yes, this is the image that visits me ... and the smile that brings me back to the simple, soft realm of Bawa ... and of Truth.

Ahsiya Posner, age 25

---

*mother Ahsiya

Being in Bawa's room now fills me with a sense of peace and serenity. It quiets my mind so that I can hear my heart speak. As a child I liked being in Bawa's room during the quiet times, not when the room was open and filled but when he was sitting and chatting with people or watching a movie. He was sweet and loving and funny. He loved to tease people. I have so many memories of those quiet moments and they always remind me of how much I loved him and how much he loved each and every one of his children.

Prashanthi Ganesan Bivins, age 31

Although I don't recall asking any questions, I knew that being in Bawa's room was the place I could go if I ever really needed to know something. I was too shy to ask a question but if I sat and listened to his discourse, the answer to my question would come. Even now, if I really feel I need to know something, I just go and sit in Bawa's room and pray.

Khary Bivins, age 28

Here is a description of what it was like to spend time in Bawa's room and to ask him a question.

I guess there was a mixture of emotions. Of course, as a kid in an environment that was so edified ... Sitting in Bawa's room, I used to feel excitement, wonder, and awe, balanced by a sense of peace. I used to rush to get the closest seat I could find. In fact, I used to go up to his room at times when it wasn't "open" hoping to slip in and spend some time around Bawa when he was "out of the spotlight." I guess I may have been hoping to observe something miraculous, or even just to "catch some fruit falling near the tree."

When I asked a question, it was partially because I really wanted to ask a question (any question) that I had thought about for a while to which I really wanted to answer.

Over the years since, I have thought a lot about that Q& A, and I have appreciated the truth in Bawa's response more and more.

Carlos (Michael) Bivins, age 32

Sitting in front of Bawa as a small child was like going to a secret place full of magical gifts, and each gift had so many layers of beauty that its strength and value has only increased with each passing year.

Bawa was soft like an angel. To go up to put one's arms around him was the best part of the day. I wouldn't wash my face after his kiss because I wanted to hold onto it right there on my cheek.

Bawa would always give us candy and apples and oranges. The candy has continued to come, and each time he throws or puts a piece of candy in our hands, it is breathtaking. He showed us his role as the bestower—illuminating God's love, sweetness, kindness and compassion, and he left his heart open for us to go into when our inside world turns harsh.

It is a secret world he gave to his children. He showed us how to catch his candy and savor its taste.

Nadine Kjellberg, age 30

Bawa Muhaiyaddeen was a rare jewel in this world. His life was devoted to serving God and his disciples, whom he referred to as "his children." He was an omniscient sage, a caring grandfather and a best friend. He was wise, yet humble. He was a teacher, yet a student. He embraced everyone and rejected no one. He had no religion, yet accepted all religions. Every act he performed was with love, and in each of his actions there was something to be learned. Bawa showed me how to live my life—with God's beautiful qualities. Through his pure faith, love, compassion, gratitude, sincerity, honesty, and selflessness, Bawa brought happiness and inner peace to all lives. Although Bawa left his physical form many years ago, his spirit grows stronger in me each day.

Jerahme Posner, age 27

786. First, let me begin by telling you that I have a really hard time putting things about Bawa into words. If I could let you into my heart to see him there, that would truly be the way to know. So, by writing about my feelings, I can only let you peek through the keyhole into my heart where he lives.

We began coming to the Fellowship when I was five years old.

In the time that has passed since (28 years — I am dating myself!), my memories and feelings and reflections all blend into warm imageries. I can't really remember the first time that I met Bawa, he was just always there. As a child, his presence filled his entire room and the surrounding house with the feeling of such warmth and security—the feeling that there really was somebody watching out for you. So strong was that feeling that it surrounded you even when you weren't at the Fellowship, or even when he was away in Ceylon. Throughout my growing years, I found comfort and safety when I felt down by simply going into Bawa's room and sitting behind the bed (in that safe little space between the bed and the wall which placed Bawa between you and everything that could possibly affect you). From five to twenty, he greeted me each time I arrived as if I had been gone a long time (even if it had only been a day)—greeting me with warmth, love, happiness, and CANDY. Sometimes, when I was a teenager, I would stray from the warmth and safety of the room and the advice of my parents and do something I would end up regretting. I would dread going into Bawa's room, feeling as if he knew everything (even if my parents, etc. did not) and would brace myself for the worst. Still, I would walk into the room and receive my warm greeting and my candy! Soon I began to realize that Bawa and God had instilled the beating I was expecting from Bawa deep within my heart and soul. I had beaten myself up so badly in expectation of what Bawa was going to say, that he had nothing left to do but comfort me. In this way, I seemed to develop a deeper sense of right and wrong which will hopefully carry me through the rest of my life, help me to become a better person and help to prepare me for being a parent myself. By the grace of God, and by the love of our father Bawa Muhaiyaddeen and his teachings, I will continue to grow and to learn.

One thing that I can tell you from the talks that Bawa gave was that it was very hard as a child to sit still, pay attention and absorb. The thing that I found which still stays with me today are the analogies he used. The visual pictures he built in your head that slowly made their way into your heart (the rose of the heart, the boat of wisdom, the dog of desire)—it helped to make things a little more real and later the analogies would translate into wisdom (hopefully, one can never be too sure).

A dream that I had years after Bawa passed away: He was sitting on the floor next to the bed, watching TV. I was going to leave the room by walking to the door by passing behind him. As I passed behind him, he reached up with his hand and gestured for me to stoop down and put my face in his hand. I woke up, and felt the touch of his hand on my face (and in my heart) for days afterwards.

Some imageries that I have from growing up with Bawa: late night snacks made up of ? inch cubes of mango, tidbits of popcorn, sugar-coated almonds; Bawa's soft palms and scratchy kisses; movies my parents' would never have let me watch outside of the room; his baby-talk voice for the little ones—*Epidi ah, shina pulei?*—in fact, I used to talk to David and Noah when they were still in my tummy like that; my love you my children, my grandchildren, my great grandchildren; how he laughed when something on TV was funny or when he heard a joke.

Lisa DeLeon, age 35

He broke everything down so we could get a better understanding of how things are.

Realized that the teaching we've been given was meant for us to see the animal nature within us and become a human being.

Gave me a better appreciation of nature and love for all God's creations, how it is and should be. He also gave me a greater appreciation of God's artistry.

Bawa's teaching helped me grow up without any kind of racism, because he explained how we are all the same inside despite the fact that we come from different backgrounds.

His teachings made it easier for me to learn about Islamic teachings when I really decided to study Islam.

Explained to me about the various energies and forces that exist in the world and how they can overtake you and make you suffer for engaging in them.

Gave me a belief in the unseen and a better understanding of how God's blessings work in the world.

He explained the History of the world as God's History.

Bawa gave me love, had and talked about Unity a lot and how important it is.

Bawa told me that I had to be good, for one day I had to free the slaves.

He told me that I had to be like the prophet David, when he committed a fault, he asked God to forgive him, and never committed that fault again.

David Nigro, age 22

Growing up with Bawa Muhaiyaddeen, I'm learning, is a unique experience unlike any other. When I was a kid, I knew he was always there for me; it wasn't something I really doubted. However, I was very shy and so I never went up to Bawa's bed or chair without my mom. I was not one of those kids who asked Bawa questions at meetings. I did, however, dream about him somewhat regularly and that was where and when I talked to Bawa. The older I got, the more I wanted to be "normal" like my school friends, so I stopped attending my nighttime meetings with Bawa. I started to forget how to connect with him. After a while, I started to feel sad and left out, it seemed like almost everyone I knew had asked Bawa questions when he was here in form. In college I started listening to his discourses and reading his books regularly. I started to connect again. I was excited to feel connected to his teachings once more. After all, it is his teachings which are important and not the man himself. I soon discovered that in order to keep that connection, I needed to pray, do *zikr* and have good qualities—or to at least have that intention. After all, I'm only a human-in-training and that leaves room for mess-ups.

Bawa's teachings are important to me because his explanations and instructions vibrate and resonate within me unlike anyone else's. Being raised in the Bawa Muhaiyaddeen Fellowship was somewhat difficult because it wasn't a choice and yet all the adults insisted that Bawa spoke the truth, which is rare. After a while, it all sounded like "blah, blah, blah". Now, after seeing my other possibilities, I'm choosing to be with Bawa.

Harmony Chelsvig, age 23

Glossary

The following traditional supplications in Arabic calligraphy are used throughout the text:

⊕ following the Prophet Muhammad or *Rasūlullāh* stands for *sallallāhu 'alaihi wa sallam,* may the blessings and peace of Allah be upon him.

⊚ following the name of a prophet or an angel stands for *'alaihis-salām,* peace be upon him.

⊛ following the name of a companion of the Prophet Muhammad, a saint, or *khalīfah* stands for *radiyallāhu 'anhu* or *'anhā,* may Allah be pleased with him or her.

(A) Indicates an Arabic word

(T) Indicates a Tamil word

'abd (A) Slave; slave of God; one who is completely surrendered to God.

adi (T) Hit; beat.

agnānam (T) Ignorance; worldly or materialistic wisdom; ignorance of the truth, of what is lasting, or eternal.

ākhirah (A) The hereafter; the next world; the divine world; the kingdom of God.

'ālam (A) (pl. *'ālamīn)* World; universe.

al-hamdu lillāh (A) All praise is to Allah. Allah is the glory and greatness that deserves all praise. "You are the One responsible for the appearance of all creations. Whatever appears, whatever disappears, whatever receives benefit or loss—all is Yours. I have surrendered everything into Your hands. I remain with hands outstretched, spread out, empty, and helpless. Whatever is happening and whatever is going to happen is all Yours."

Allāhu or Allah (A) God; the One and Only; the One of infinite grace and incomparable love; the One who gives of His undiminishing wealth of grace; the One who is beyond comparison or example; the Eternal, Effulgent One; the One of overpowering effulgence.

Allāhu akbar (A) God is great!

Allāhu ta'ālā Nāyan (A & T) God is the Lord above all. *Allāhu* (A) Almighty God; *ta'ālā* (A) the One who exists in all lives in a state of humility and exaltedness; *Nāyan* (T) the Ruler who protects and sustains.

Āmīn (A) So be it. May God make this complete; may it be so.

anāthi (T) The beginningless beginning; the state in which God was alone, meditating upon Himself; the period before creation when Allah was alone in darkness, unaware of Himself, even though everything was within Him; the state of unmanifestation, before the creation came forth.

anbu (T) Love.

arwāh (A) (sing. *rūh)* The divine realm; heaven; the world of pure souls; the period in which the souls were manifested. Lit. souls.

as-salāmu 'alaikum (A) "May the peace and peacefulness of Allah be upon you." This is a greeting of love. *As-salāmu 'alaikum, wa 'alaikumus-salām.* One heart embraces the other with love and greets it with respect and honor. Both hearts are one. In reply, *wa 'alaikumus-salām* means, "May the peace and peacefulness of Allah be upon you also."

as-salāmu 'alaikum wa rahmatullāhi wa barakātuhu kulluhu (A) May all the peace, the beneficence, and the blessings of God be upon you.

astaghfirullāhal-'azīm (A) O Allah, forgive all our faults and correct us. I seek forgiveness from Allah, the Supreme.

āthi or *Āthi* (T) Primal beginning; the period after *anāthi* (the beginningless beginning); the time when the *Nūr* (the plenitude of the light of Allah) and the *Qutb* (the wisdom which explains the truth of God) manifested within Allah; the time of the dawning of the light; the world of grace where the unmanifested begins to manifest in the form of resonance. In contrast to *awwal,* when the creations became manifest in form, *āthi* is the time when the first sound or vibration emerged. *Āthi* also refers to Allah, the Primal, Original One.

a'udhu billāhi minash-shaitānir-rajīm (A) I seek refuge in Allah from the evils of the accursed satan. "Please annihilate satan from within me. Eliminate him from within me and burn him up. *Minal* (T) is the fire of the resplendent light that comes like lightning. In the same way that lightning strikes, burn him away from me. Burn satan who is the enemy to the children of Adam ☻. He is the one who has separated us from You, O God. Please prevent that enemy from coming and mingling within us. Prevent him from coming once again into our midst, and take us back to You."

auliyā' (A) (sing. *walī*) The favorites of God; those who are near to God; commonly used to refer to holy ones of Islam.

awwal (A) The time of the creation of forms; the stage at which the soul became surrounded by form and each creation took shape; the stage at which the souls of the six kinds of lives (earth life, fire life, water life, air life, ether life, and light life) were placed in their respective forms. Allah created these forms and then placed that entrusted treasure *(amānah)* which is the soul within those forms.

Bismillāhir-Rahmānir-Rahīm (A) In the name of God, Most Merciful, Most Compassionate.
　Bismillāh: Allah, the first and the last; the One with a beginning and without a beginning. He is the One who is the cause for creation and for the absence of creation, the cause for the beginning and for the beginningless. He is the One who is completeness.
　ar-Rahmān: He is the King, the Compassionate One, and the Beneficent One. He is the One who protects all creations and gives them nourishment. He looks after them, gives them love, takes them unto Himself, and comforts them. He gives them food, houses, property, and everything within Himself. He holds His creations within Himself and protects them. He is the One who reigns with justice.
　ar-Rahīm: He is the One who redeems, the One who protects us from evil, the One who preserves and confers eternal bliss. No matter what we may do, He has the quality of forgiving us and accepting us back. He is the Tolerant One who forgives all the faults we have committed. He is the Savior. On the Day of Judgment, on the Day of Inquiry, and on all days since the beginning, He protects and brings His creations back unto Himself.

Bismin (A) A shortened form of *Bismillāhir-Rahmānir-Rahīm*.

chee (T) Tamil expression of disgust.

dēva(s) (T) Celestial being.

dhikr (A) The remembrance of God. It is a common name given to traditional prayers in praise of God. Of the many *dhikrs*, the most exalted *dhikr* is to say, "*Lā ilāha illallāhu:* There is nothing other than You, O God. Only You are Allah." All the other *dhikrs* relate to His actions *(wilāyāt),* but this *dhikr* points to Him and to Him alone. It is the *dhikr* of Allah's *'arsh* (throne). *See also kalimah; Lā ilāha illallāhu.*

dunyā (A) The earth-world in which we live; the world of physical existence; the darkness which separated from Allah at the time when the light of the *Nūr Muhammad* manifested from within Allah.

ēmāttam (T) Deception.

Fātihah (A) *Sūratul-Fātihah,* the opening chapter of the Qur'an.

Furqān (A) The religion or scripture of Islam, corresponding to the fourth step of spiritual ascendance. *Furqān* was revealed to Moses ☮ and Muhammad ☮. It is the "criterion" which distinguishes between good and evil, right and wrong, lawful and unlawful, truth and illusion. This is the region of the head and the seven openings (two eyes, two ears, two nostrils, and one mouth), through which man receives explanations. *See also Injīl; Jabrāt, Zabūr.*

gnānam (T) Divine wisdom. If a person can throw away all the worldly wealth and take within him only the treasure called Allah and His qualities and actions, His conduct and behavior, if he makes Allah the only treasure and completeness for him—that is the state of *gnānam.*

gnāni (T) A gnostic; one who has divine wisdom, or *gnānam,* one who has received the qualities and wisdom of God by surrendering to God, and, having received these, lives in a state of peace where he sees all lives as equal; one who has attained the state of peace.

guru (T) A divinely wise spiritual teacher or guide; a *shaikh.*

hajj (A) The holy pilgrimage to Mecca; the fifth *fard* (obligatory duty) in Islam. This duty must be done wearing the white shroud *(kafan),* signifying that one has died to the world. Before undertaking this pilgrimage, one's wealth must be shared among the poor. A person with a spouse and children must divide his wealth among them. The inner pilgrimage is to enter the state of dying before death. The inner desires must be surrendered and all of the self must die to make this pilgrimage.

halāl (A) Permissible; those things that are permissible or lawful according to the commands of God and which conform to the word of God.

harām (A) Forbidden; impermissible; that which is forbidden by truth, justice, and the commands of God. For those who are on the straight path, *harām* means all the evil things, actions, food, and dangers that can obstruct the path.

hayawān(s) (A) Beast.

houri(s) This is an Anglicized word derived from the Arabic word *hūrīya* meaning celestial beings.

idi (T) Hit; beat.

illallāh(u) (A) Nothing other than Allah. The second part of the *dhikr*, which accompanies the breath as it is drawn in through the right nostril and is finally deposited in the inner heart. *See also Lā ilāha illallāhu.*

'ilm (A) Knowledge; divine knowledge; that secret knowledge, or light, that shines in the heart of the truly pious, whereby one becomes enlightened.

īmān (A) Absolute, complete, and unshakable faith, certitude, and determination that God alone exists; the complete acceptance by the heart that God is One.

Injīl (A) The religion or scripture of Christianity, which corresponds to the third step of spiritual ascendance. This is the region of the chest which is filled with thoughts, emotions, spirits, and vapors. *See also Furqān; Jabrāt; Zabūr.*

insān(s) (A) Man; a human being. The true form of man is the form of Allah's qualities, actions, conduct, behavior, and virtues. The one who has realized the completeness of this form, having filled himself with these qualities, is truly an *insān*.

insān kāmil (A) A perfected, God-realized being; one who has realized Allah as his only wealth, cutting away all the wealth of the world and the wealth sought by the mind; one who has acquired God's qualities, performs his own actions accordingly, and immerses himself within those qualities.

Jabrāt (A) The religion or scripture of Zoroastrianism, or fire worship, which corresponds to the second step of spiritual ascendance. *Jabrāt* relates to hunger, disease, and old age, and is in the area of the stomach. *See also Furqān; Injīl; Zabūr.*

Ka'bah (A) The *Ka'bah*, also known as the House of God *(Baitullāh)*, is the central point toward which all Muslims turn to pray five times a day and is also the object of the pilgrimage *(hajj)*, the fifth *fard* (obligatory duty) of Islam. This cube-like building was originally built by Adam ☮ in what is now the city of Mecca and has been rebuilt numerous times throughout the ages, most notably by Prophet Abraham ☉ and his son, Prophet Ishmael ☉. The Prophet Muhammad ☉ was commanded by God to cleanse the *Ka'bah* of all idols and to restore its original purity and sanctity.

Within the human being, the *Ka'bah* represents the heart *(qalb)*, the original source of prayer. It is the place in which a true human being meets God face to face. Like the outer *Ka'bah*, this sanctuary, too, must be cleansed of idols and restored to its original purity as the house in which God abides.

kalimah (A) The affirmation of faith—*Lā ilāha illallāhu:* There is nothing other than You, O God. Only You are Allah. The recitation or remembrance of God which cuts away the influence of the five elements (earth, fire, water, air, and ether), washes away all the *karma* that has accumulated from the very beginning until now, dispels the darkness, beautifies the heart, and makes it resplend. The *kalimah* washes the body and the heart of man and makes him pure, makes his wisdom emerge, and impels that wisdom to know the self and God. *See also dhikr; Lā ilāha illallāhu.*

Karbalā' (A) When Allah ordered the Angel 'Izrā'īl ☉ to take a handful of earth, from which Adam ☉ was created, that handful of earth gathered from all four directions was placed in *Karbalā'*, the center of the eighteen thousand universes.

It is also a city located in Iraq, which throughout the ages has been a battlefield. It is where al-Hussain ☉, the son of 'Alī ☉, fought against his enemies and was killed. On a symbolic level, *Karbalā'* signifies the battlefield of the heart *(qalb)*.

karma (T) The inherited qualities formed at the time of conception; the qualities of the essence of the five elements; the qualities of the mind; the qualities of the connection to hell.

khair (A) That which is right or good; that which is acceptable to wisdom and to Allah, as opposed to *sharr*, that which is evil or bad.

kursī (A) The gnostic eye; the eye of light; the center of the forehead where Allah's resplendence *(Nūr)* was impressed on Adam's ☉ forehead. Lit. stool or seat.

Lā ilāha (A) There is nothing other than You.

Lā ilāha illallāh(u) (A) There is nothing other than You, O God. Only You are Allah. To accept this with certitude, to strengthen one's unshakable faith *(īmān)*, and to affirm this *kalimah* is the state of Islam.

There are two aspects. *Lā ilāha* is the manifestation of creation *(sifāt)*. *Illallāhu* is the essence *(dhāt)*. All that has appeared, all creation, belongs to *lā ilāha*. The name of the One who created all that is *illallāhu*. Lit. No god (is), except the One God. *See also dhikr; kalimah.*

Lā ilāha illallāh Muhammadur-Rasūlullāh (A) There is nothing other than You, O God. Only You are Allah and Muhammad is the Messenger of God.

malā'ikat (A) (sing. *malak*) Archangels. Lit. angels.

mal'ūn (A) Accursed, rejected; a name attributed to satan.

māyā (T) Illusion; the unreality of the visible world; the glitters seen in the darkness of illusion; the 105 million glitters seen in the darkness of the mind which result in 105 million rebirths. *Māyā* is an energy, or *sakthi*, which takes on various shapes, causes man to forfeit his wisdom, and confuses and hypnotizes him into a state of torpor. It can take many, many millions of hypnotic forms. If man tries to grasp one of these forms with his intellect, although he sees the form he will never catch it, for it will elude him by taking on yet another form.

Maya veeram (T) The strength of illusion.

meignānam (T) True wisdom.

mīm (A) The Arabic letter (م) which corresponds to the English consonant 'm'. In the transformed man of wisdom, *mīm* represents Muhammad ☮. The shape of *mīm* is like a sperm cell and from this comes the *nuqtah*, or dot, which is the form of the world.

nafs (A) The seven kinds of base desires; that is, desires meant to satisfy one's own pleasure and comfort. Lit. person; spirit; inclination or desire which goads or incites toward evil.

Nūr (A) Light; the resplendence of Allah; the plenitude of the light of Allah, which has the brilliance of a hundred million suns; the completeness of Allah's qualities. When the plenitude of all these becomes one and resplends as one, that is the *Nūr*, that is Allah's qualities and His beauty. It is the resplendent wisdom that is innate in man and can be awakened.

Nūr Muhammad (A) The beauty of the qualities and actions of the powers *(wilāyāt)* of Allah, the radiance of Allah's essence *(dhāt)* which shines within the resplendence of His truth. It was the light of Muhammad ☮ called *Nūr Muhammad* that was impressed upon the forehead of Adam ☮.

Of the nine aspects of Muhammad ☙, *Nūr Muhammad* is that aspect which is Allah's wisdom.

olis (T) Lights of God; illumined beings.

pee matham (T) Fecal arrogance.

poignānam (T) False wisdom.

Purānas (T) Stories, usually referring to the Hindu scriptures; mythologies; legends; epics. The stories of each religion can be described as *purānas*. Some were sent down as commandments from God, others were created through man's intelligence and senses, while still others were created by poets, usually as songs of praise depicting stories.

Bawa Muhaiyaddeen ☙ speaks of the seventeen *purānas* within man as the qualities of arrogance, *karma*, and *māyā;* the three sons of *māyā* *(tārahan, singhan,* and *sūran);* desire, anger, miserliness, attachment, fanaticism, envy; intoxicants, lust, theft, murder, and falsehood.

qalb (A) Heart; the heart within the heart of man; the innermost heart. Bawa Muhaiyaddeen ☙ explains that there are two states for the *qalb*. In one state the *qalb* is made up of four chambers, which are earth, fire, air, and water—representing Hinduism, fire worship, Christianity, and Islam. Inside these four chambers is the second state, the flower of the *qalb* which is the divine qualities of God. This is the flower of grace *(rahmat)*. God's fragrance exists within this inner *qalb*.

Qiyāmah (A) The Day of Standing Forth; Day of Reckoning; Day of Questioning.

qudrat (A) Power; the power of God's grace and the qualities which control all other forces.

Quls (A) A reference to the last three *sūrats* in the Qur'an: *Sūratul-Ikhlās, Sūratul-Falaq,* and *Sūratun-Nās*.

qurbān (A) Externally, it is a ritual method for the slaughter of animals in order to purify them and make them permissible, or *halāl,* to eat. Inwardly, it is to purify one's heart *(qalb)* by sacrificing and cutting away the animal qualities existing within oneself, thus making one's life *halāl*. The *Subhānallāhi Kalimah* was revealed for the purpose of destroying these animal qualities within the *qalb*.

Qutb ☙ or *qutb(s)* (A) One who functions in the state of divine analytic wisdom *(pahuth arivu),* the sixth level of consciousness. The one who, having measured the length and breadth of the seven oceans of the base desires, raises up the ship of life that lies buried in the ocean of *māyā*, and rescues it from that ocean.

ar-Rahmān (A) The Most Gracious, Most Merciful. *Ar-Rahmān*—one of the ninety-nine beautiful names *(al-asmā'ul-husnā)* of Allah. The One who rules is forever ruling with His three thousand compassionate, benevolent qualities. He has no anger at all. His duty is only to protect and sustain.

Rasūl ☥ (A) The Messenger of Allah, Prophet Muhammad ☥; God's essence *(dhāt)*, the resplendence that emerged from His effulgence, shining radiantly as His Messenger ☥. Muhammad ☥, the manifestation of that resplendence, discourses on the explanations of luminous wisdom, which he imparts to Allah's creations. He is the one who begs for truth from Allah and intercedes with prayers for all of Allah's creations and for his followers. Therefore, Allah has anointed His *Rasūl*, the Prophet Muhammad ☥, with the title: *The Messenger who is the savior for both worlds.* The word *rasūl* can be used to refer to any of Allah's apostles or messengers.

Rasūlullāh ☥ (A) The Messenger of Allah; a title used for Prophet Muhammad ☥.

Razzāq (A) *Ar-Razzāq*, the Provider; one of the ninety-nine beautiful names *(al-asmā'ul-husnā)* of Allah.

rūh (A) The soul; the light ray of God; the light of God's wisdom. Bawa Muhaiyaddeen ☥ explains that *rūh* is life *(hayāt)*. Out of the six kinds of lives it is the light life, the human life. It is a ray of the light of the resplendence of Allah (the *Nūr*), a ray that does not die or disappear. It is the truth. The other five lives appear and disappear. That which exists forever without death is the soul. It is Allah's grace *(rahmat)*, which has obtained the wealth of the imperishable treasure of all three worlds *(mubārakāt)*.

rupee(s) (T) Unit of money in Sri Lanka and India.

sabūr (A) Inner patience. Patience is Allah's treasure chest. Going within this treasure chest, reflecting and having forbearance is *sabūr*. It is the first of the four qualities of *sabūr, shakūr, tawakkul,* and *al-hamdu lillāh*—inner patience, contentment, trust in God, and all praise is to God.

saivam (T) Inner purity. In common usage it refers to the religion of Hinduism and to vegetarianism.

sakthi (T) Elemental energy; force.

sallallāhu 'alaihi wa sallam (A) God bless him and grant him peace. A supplication traditionally spoken after mentioning the name of Prophet Muhammad ☮. In text usually denoted with Arabic calligraphy.

sanīsvaran (T) A name for satan.

sārī (T) Traditional clothing for women of India and nearby countries consisting of six yards of fabric draped into a modest dress and head covering.

shaikh (A) A spiritual guide or master; one, who knowing himself and God, guides others on the straight path, the path to God.

shakūr (A) Gratitude; contentment with whatever may happen, realizing that everything comes from Allah; contentment arising from gratitude; the state within the inner patience known as *sabūr*; that which is stored within the treasure chest of patience.

sharr (A) That which is wrong, bad, or evil, as opposed to *khair*, that which is good.

tārahan, singhan, and *sūran* (T) The three sons of illusion *(māyā)*.

tatthwas (T) Potentialities; the strength or vitality inherent in the qualities of the creations, manifested through the actions of each of those qualities.

tawakkul (A) Absolute trust in God; surrender to God; handing over to God the entire responsibility for everything.

tholuhai (T) Prayer; the five-times prayer of Islam.

vingnānam (T) Scientific wisdom.

wahy (A) Revelation; inspiration from God; the inspired word of God revealed to a prophet; the commandments or words of God transmitted by the Archangel Gabriel ☮. *Wahys*, or revelations, have come to Adam ☮, Moses ☮, and various other prophets, but especially to Prophet Muhammad ☮. Muhammad ☮ received 6,666 revelations. The histories of each of the earlier prophets were contained within the revelations given to Prophet Muhammad ☮.

wilāyat (pl. *wilāyāt*) (A) God's power; that which has been revealed and manifested through God's actions; the miraculous names and actions of God; the powers of His attributes through which all creations came into existence.

Yā (A) The vocative 'O!'. An exclamation of praise; a title of greatness or praise.

Zabūr (A) *Zabūr* is the scripture corresponding to Hinduism, which relates to the creation of form, the appearance of man. In the body, Hinduism relates to the area below the waist. *See also Furqān; Injīl; Jabrāt.*

Questions by Topic

ANGELS

How does the heart move? And why can't you see the angels?	56
Why can't we see the angels on our shoulders?	69
How does God create angels?	100

ANIMALS/PETS

Talk to a child mourning his pet squirrel.	3
Is there an animal heaven?	17

BAWA MUHAIYADDEEN

How did Bawa get so wise?	53
How do you know what people are thinking?	58
When Bawa feels better can I sit on his lap?	111
Does God tell Bawa what to say, or does he just know?	124

BIRTH AND DEATH

A young child asks about where he came from and about death.	21
Why did we choose to come here when we were already part of God to begin with?	40
When babies die, do they go to heaven or hell?	81
What happens when you die?	85
After a person dies and goes to hell, is it still possible for them to repent and go to heaven?	133
Why did we come to this world, if the world of the soul was so good?	151

COMPASSION

Talk to a child mourning his pet squirrel.	3

CONDUCT

Advice to a young boy on how to conduct his life.	11
What is the proper conduct between boys and girls ten years to eighteen years old?	31
I am ten years old and am wondering if it is proper to wear make-up.	32
What is wrong with dancing? Does that include ballet, tap, and dancing one does by oneself?	33
If we can't go dancing or play with boys, what can we do for fun?	36
At what age do you think boys and girls should date, and at what age can boys and girls leave home?	55
Is rock and roll bad for you?	55
How does God take you to heaven or hell?	74
What happened to Adam ☮ when satan spat on him?	79
Listen my children.	91
Is it good to give salāms *(greetings of peace) to people in passing?*	95
When you do the same bad thing again and ask for forgiveness, will God forgive you again?	109
When I hear bad words, I try to get them out of my mind, but they don't really go out sometimes, so what should I do?	110
Satan used to be good, so how could he be so bad now?	112
How do I find God?	117
Why did Judas think that Jesus ☮ was bad?	129
After a person dies and goes to hell, is it still possible for them to repent and go to heaven?	133
How do you chase away fear?	137
How can we get our son up for early morning prayer?	139
How do you get over laziness?	149
Could Bawa comment on children who just sit during early morning prayer but don't recite anything.	160
How do I show my son that the treasures of God are more fulfilling than the things he wants in this world?	164

CONTEMPORARY WORLD

Advice to a young boy on how to conduct his life.	11

What is the proper conduct between boys and girls ten years to eighteen years old?	*31*
I am ten years old and am wondering if it is proper to wear make-up.	*32*
What is wrong with dancing? Does that include ballet, tap, and dancing one does by oneself?	*33*
If we can't go dancing or play with boys, what can we do for fun?	*36*
At what age you think boys and girls should date, and at what age can boys and girls leave home?	*55*
Is rock and roll bad for you?	*55*
Why is the world always hard?	*69*
Listen my children.	*91*
If someone teases you for not eating meat, what should you do?	*157*
How do I show my son that the treasures of God are more fulfilling than the things he wants in this world?	*164*

CREATION

Are there other people in outer space?	*41*
How did God make the first person alive?	*75*
How did satan create demons?	*95*
How does God create angels?	*100*
How was God made?	*101*
Why did God make the other planets if no one lives on them?	*105*
Why did God create satan?	*113*
How come God made satan?	*121*
Did God create heaven?	*122*
How come God made people?	*137*
How did God create the world?	*140*
If there were no God, who would create us?	*145*
Why did we come to this world, if the world of the soul was so good?	*151*

DREAMS

How do you chase away scary dreams?	*138*

DUTY

What type of Fellowship work can the children do to feel a part of it?   46

ENERGIES/ELEMENTS

Is there an animal heaven?   17

How does the heart move? And why can't you see the angels?   56

FEAR

How do you chase away fear?   137

FELLOWSHIP

How do we handle what our friends think about our Arabic names? People don't understand why we don't just go to a church or a synagogue like other people. How do we explain to them about the Fellowship?   37

What type of Fellowship work can the children do to feel a part of it?   46

FORGIVENESS

When you do the same bad thing again and ask for forgiveness, will God forgive you again?   109

After a person dies and goes to hell, is it still possible for them to repent and go to heaven?   133

FRIENDSHIP

How do we handle what our friends think about our Arabic names? People don't understand why we don't just go to a church or a synagogue like other people. How do we explain to them about the Fellowship?   37

What should I tell my friends who told me God is just pretend. What should I tell them?   43

GOD

What does Bawa mean when he says God was never born and can never die? How did God come to exist then?   44

If God has no beginning or end, how did He get here?	53
Why did God make satan if He wanted us to be good?	57
How can God be in everybody's heart if He is only one?	57
How does God take you to heaven or hell?	74
How did God make the first person alive?	75
How did God destroy satan? Can God destroy satan with His fire?	84
How does God create angels?	100
If God is One, how could He be in everyone's heart?	100
How was God made?	101
Why did God make the other planets if no one lives on them?	105
When you do the same bad thing again and ask for forgiveness, will God forgive you again?	109
We know that God will always exist forever, but will satan always exist forever?	110
Why did God create satan?	113
How do I find God?	117
How come God made satan?	121
Did God create heaven?	122
If satan was not here, would God be here?	124
How come God made people?	137
How did God create the world?	140
If there were no God, who would create us?	145
Why did we come to this world, if the world of the soul was so good?	151

HAJJ

How can I go to Mecca?	59

HEART

How does the heart move? And why can't you see the angels?	56
How can God be in everybody's heart if He is only one?	57
How do you get to God?	81
If God is One, how could He be in everyone's heart?	100

HEAVEN AND HELL

What does heaven look like?	*39*
If you go to hell, what feels the pain if you don't have your body?	*39*
How does God take you to heaven or hell?	*74*
When babies die, do they go to heaven or hell?	*81*
How do you get to hell or heaven?	*85*
Does satan take you to hell?	*86*
We know that God will always exist forever, but will satan always exist forever?	*110*
Did God create heaven?	*122*
After a person dies and goes to hell, is it still possible for them to repent and go to heaven?	*133*

LANGUAGES

How do we handle what our friends think about our Arabic names? People don't understand why we don't just go to a church or a synagogue like other people. How do we explain to them about the Fellowship?	*37*
Is there any benefit in studying Arabic?	*155*

MAN

Why did we choose to come here when we were already part of God to begin with?	*40*
How did God make the first person alive?	*75*
How do you get to God?	*81*
If you see God, do you see Him with your own eyes?	*83*
How do you destroy satan?	*84*
Does satan take you to hell?	*86*
How do I find God?	*117*
After a person dies and goes to hell, is it still possible for them to repent and go to heaven?	*133*
How do you chase away fear?	*137*
How come God made people?	*137*

If there were no God, who would create us?	145
Why did we come to this world, if the world of the soul was so good?	151

PARENTING

How can we get our son up for early morning prayer?	139
Could Bawa comment on children who just sit during early morning prayer but don't recite anything.	160
Every time I want a toy, is that blocking my surrender to God?	163
How do I show my son that the treasures of God are more fulfilling than the things he wants in this world?	164

PERSONAL LIFE

Advice to a young boy on how to conduct his life.	11
What is the proper conduct between boys and girls ten years to eighteen years old?	31
I am ten years old and am wondering if it is proper to wear make-up.	32
What is wrong with dancing? Does that include ballet, tap, and dancing one does by oneself?	33
If we can't go dancing or play with boys, what can we do for fun?	36
At what age do you think boys and girls should date, and at what age can boys and girls leave home?	55
Is rock and roll bad for you?	55
Is it good to give salāms *(greetings of peace) to people in passing?*	95
How can we get our son up for early morning prayer?	139
How do you get over laziness?	149
Is there any benefit in studying Arabic?	155
If someone teases you for not eating meat, what should you do?	157
What prayer should I recite before a test?	159
Could Bawa comment on children who just sit during early morning prayer but don't recite anything.	160
How do I show my son that the treasures of God are more fulfilling than the things he wants in this world?	164

PRAYER

Can Bawa give me a special prayer to say?	65
Is it good to give salāms (greetings of peace) to people in passing?	95
How can we get our son up for early morning prayer?	139
What prayer should I recite before a test?	159
Could Bawa comment on children who just sit during early morning prayer but don't recite anything.	160

PROPHETS

If Adam and Eve ☮ had obeyed God, would the whole world still be a garden of Eden?	38
What happened to Adam ☮ when satan spat on him?	79
Why did Judas think that Jesus ☮ was bad?	129
How did God create the world?	140

RELIGION

How do we handle what our friends think about our Arabic names? People don't understand why we don't just go to a church or a synagogue like other people. How do we explain to them about the Fellowship?	37
What should I say when somebody asks me what religion I am?	73
How do you get to God?	81
If someone teases you for not eating meat, what should you do?	157

SATAN

Why did God make satan if He wanted us to be good?	57
Why has God chosen for satan to be evil?	60
What happened to Adam ☮ when satan spat on him?	79
How do you destroy satan?	84
How did God destroy satan? Can God destroy satan with His fire?	84
Does satan take you to hell?	86
How did satan create demons?	95

We know that God will always exist forever, but will satan always exist forever?	*110*
Satan used to be good, so how could he be so bad now?	*112*
Why did God create satan?	*113*
How come God made satan?	*121*
How come satan is bad?	*122*
If satan was not here, would God be here?	*124*

SPIRITUAL PATH

Why did we choose to come here when we were already part of God to begin with?	*40*
Why is the world always hard?	*69*
What should I say when somebody asks me what religion I am?	*73*
How do you get to God?	*81*
If you see God, do you see Him with your own eyes?	*83*
How do you destroy satan?	*84*
Listen my children.	*91*
How do I find God?	*117*
How do you get over laziness?	*149*
Why did we come to this world, if the world of the soul was so good?	*151*
In Maya Veeram, why do you call it the ABCD world?	*169*

WORLD

Why did we choose to come here when we were already part of God to begin with?	*40*
Are there other people in outer space?	*41*
Why is the world always hard?	*69*
Listen my children.	*91*
How did God create the world?	*140*
Why did we come to this world, if the world of the soul was so good?	*151*
How does day change into night?	*160*
In Maya Veeram, why do you call it the ABCD world?	*169*

Index

ABCD world, 169–170
Abū, when—spat on Adam ☮ and became satan, 121, 140
Adam ☮
 and Eve ☮, 38–39
 satan spat on, 121, 140
agreement for life span, 3–7
al-hamdu lillāh, see God, praise of
aliens, *see* outer space
angels, why can't I see—?, 56, 69–70
anger, 13, 57
animal(s)
 avoid trampling people, 23
 bathing in mud, 161
 behavior and human behavior, 23, 112
 heaven, 17–18
Arabic, benefit of studying, 155–157
atoms, cutting, 123–125

baby of heart, 117
bathroom, clean self afterwards, 17–18
Bawa Muhaiyaddeen, *see* Muhaiyaddeen, Bawa
beauty of the world, 93–94
behavior, animal and human, 17–18, 23
beings exist in all places, 105–106
betray, we—God, 129
birth, reason for, 40–41
Bismillāhir-Rahmānir-Rahīm, 159
 say, 11–13
blind man and lamp, 43–44
blood ties, effect of, 24
body, inner, *see* three bodies
body, outer, *see* three bodies

book of life, 47
buffalo stirs up mud, 161

cat washing its face, 117
children
 advice for, 112–113
 asking subtle questions, 21, 22, 25
 God teaches through, 21, 22, 23, 25–27
 know all languages, 23
 parents must correct themselves before correcting, 161–163
 pure hearts of, 22
 purity of, 21–22, 25
 remembering original knowledge, 26
 study within, 141
 unity of, 21–22
 why—are born, 25–26
 words of, 22
clean and unclean, 18
conduct for life, 12–13
conscience, 45
contentment, 13
correcting yourself, 34
creation, 137–138, 140–141
 search for reason for, 138
 through mind and desire, 140
creations, of God and man, 145–146
crop, tending, 4–5
crying for others, 3

dancing, 33–36
 with boys, 36
 with God, 34
dating, 55
day and night, 160

death, 21, 23
  attain benefit of good before our, 133
dhikr, 160, 162, *see also* prayer
  five-times prayer and, 162
  refusing to recite, 160–163
  of sufi, 162
divine analytic wisdom, protect animals without, 5–6
dreams
  body and, 39–40
  scary, 138
drugs and alcohol, 12
duty, 46
  do—correctly, 4–5

elements, 56
evil qualities are satan, 130
eye of wisdom, 42
eyes as a mirror, 41–42

father of soul, 53
father of wisdom, 58–59
  raise in your heart, 117
faults, repeating, 109–110
fear, 137
Fellowship
  answering question about, 37–38
  group that unites everyone, 74
fighting, 150
first person, creation of, 75
fish out of water like man leaving God, 105–106
flesh, do not eat, 12
flower and beetle, 31–32
food, *halāl* and *harām*, 157–158
fools, four, 170
foot, start with right, 11–12, 13
forgiveness, ask for, 27, 109–110
fragrance of God's qualities, 122
freedom of man is lost, 61–62
fruit, God is like juice within, 124
fruit tree, care for—to receive benefit, 91–92
fun, 36, 37

Gabriel ☉, 113
God
  answers you, 54
  cannot be destroyed, 111
  create—within, 124, 138
  and creation, 75
  creation by—alone, 145–146
  creation of world by, 140–141
  find treasure of—within, 105–106
  in everyone's heart, 57–58
  hand over all responsibility to, 6–7
  has no beginning or end, 53–54
  how to find, 117
  if—did not create anything, 149–150
  like a seed, 44
  many roles of, 124
  no birth or death, 44–45
  people who say—is pretend, 43–44
  power of, 123–124
  power of—goes everywhere, 58
  praise of, 13
  the Protector, 11–13
  speaking to, 24
  surrender to, 163–164
  trust in, 13
  uniting with, 24–25
  we betray, 129
  we came here to understand, 40–41
  work of, 12
golden loincloth, 36–37
good actions, 47
good and bad, 110–111

heart
  baby of, 117
  darkness in, 24
  how does—move?, 56
  secrets in, 24
  stained, like white dress, 109–110
heaven, 17, 38–39, 74–75, 122–124
  animal, 17–18
  and hell, 111
  living in kingdom of, 141
  in your life, 49

hell, 17, 39–40, 74–75, 122
  cannot repent in, 133
  and heaven, 111
  qualities of, 112
home, when children can leave, 55
house, leaving with *Bismin*, 11–12
hunger of others, 12

ignorant people, 43–44
illusion, ocean of, 11–12
inner body, *see* three bodies
intention, establishing, 11–12

jealousy and satan, 121–122
jinn(s), 57
  in bottle, 61–62
Judas, 129–130
judging others is God's work, 12
Jupiter, 105

kalimah, 73
  explanation, 65–66
kosher, *see* food, *halāl* and *harām*

Lā ilāha illallāh, Muhammadur-Rasūlullāh, *see kalimah*, explanation
language, original, 23–24
laziness, 149
life
  journey of, 11–13
  on other planets, 105–106
  span for all creation, 3–7
light and God, 58
light life, 17
lives
  receive nourishment from five elements, 3–4
  six kinds of, 17–18, 56
loincloth, golden, *see* golden loincloth

make-up, 32–33, 117
man
  becoming like satan, 112–113
  creates satan within, 122

man *(continued)*
  creations of, 145–146
  understand lives inside, 151–152
  of wisdom can return man's freedom, 61
Mars, 105
Maya Veeram, 169–170
meat
  fake, 158, *see also* flesh, do not eat
  not eating, *see* vegetarian, explaining to other children
Mecca, child asks to go to, 59–60
milk of love, 117
milk of wisdom, 117
mind, 56
  as parrot, control, 7
  enemy of our life, 48–49
mirror, father of wisdom as, 58–59
Muhaiyaddeen, Bawa
  comforts his children, 75
  crying for others, 3
  gets wisdom, 53
  sitting on—lap, 111
  source of his talking, 124–125
music
  created by God, 33–34
  rock and roll, 55

nightmares, *see* dreams, scary
ninety-nine revolving parts of atom, 123–124

ocean of illusion, 11–12
opposites, 121, 124
  exist for learning wisdom, 110–111
outer body, *see* three bodies
outer space, 41–42

paradise, *see* heaven
parent(s)
  children correcting, 25–26
  teach children wisdom, 164–165
  teaching children right and wrong, 163–165

parrot of mind, 7
peace
   achieving—of mind, 48–49
   attain—by changing qualities, 130
   kingdom of, 26–27
   not found in bars, 48, 49
   trying to find—in the world, 37
people
   ignorant, 43–44
   inside us, 41
   why created, 137–138
places, beings exist in all, 105
plane, traveling, 42
planets, 105
power, God is, 58
praise God, 13
prayer(s), 65–66
   knowing right time to pray, 159–160
   waking children for, 139–140
principle, basic, 41
prophet(s), 73, 75
   Adam and Eve ☮, 38–39
   Daoud ☮, 27
   speak about children, 22
protection, ask for God's, 11–12
purity, kingdom of, 26–27

qualities
   evil—are satan, 130
   gathering good and bad, 113
   good—needed by man, 112
   satan's, 112
questions, essential, 21–22, 23, 24
qurbān, 157

Razzaq, meaning of name, 45
religion, answering questions about, 73–74
religions, four, 73–74
research within, 105–106
right and wrong, parent teaching children, 163–165
rock and roll, 55

satan, 24, 56, 60–62
   becoming bad, 112–113, 121–122
   creates evil qualities, 140
   did not want to pray behind Adam ☮, 121
   evil qualities are, 130
   existence of, 110–111
   leader of jinns, 121
   not created by God, 113–114, 121–122
   opposite to God, 121
   qualities of, 57
   spat on Adam ☮, 121, 140
   why did God make, 57
school, life is a, 40–41
scientific research and inner research, 105–106
seeds, sow, 4–5
senses, five, 61
sexual attraction, 31–32
shakūr, *see* contentment
sin, 6
snake, poisonous fangs of, 112
sorrow, do not indulge in, 4–8
soul, 17
   father of, 53
   joined with five other lives, 151
   why—comes to this world, 151–152
souls, pure and impure, 137–138, 151
squirrel that died, 3
stars speak, 105
story, know your own and God's, 150–151
suffering of others, 12
surrender, *see* God, surrender to

tawakkul, *see* God, trust in
tests, praying before, 159–160
three bodies, 39–40
tiredness, 25
trample
   human beings—each other, 23
tree, care for—to receive benefit, 91–93

unity, 22–23, 73–74, 117
  like many-colored flower garden, 39
university of the world, 141, 152

vegetarian, explaining to other children,
    157–158, *see also* flesh, do not eat

white dress, stained, 109–110
wisdom
  divine analytic, 17–18
  do not teach—to ignorant people,
    43–44
  eye of, 42
  father of—as mirror, 58–59
  man of—can free man, 61–62
  strive to plant—and grow in our
    lives, 91–93
  understanding with, 34
  you need a father of, 117
words, bad, 110
work, 46
world is hard, 69

Other Books by M. R. Bawa Muhaiyaddeen ☉

Truth & Light: brief explanations
Songs of God's Grace
The Divine Luminous Wisdom That Dispels the Darkness
Wisdom of the Divine (Vols. 1–5)
The Guidebook to the True Secret of the Heart (Vols. 1, 2)
God, His Prophets and His Children
Four Steps to Pure Iman
The Wisdom of Man
A Book of God's Love
My Love You My Children: 101 Stories for Children of All Ages
Come to the Secret Garden: Sufi Tales of Wisdom
The Golden Words of a Sufi Sheikh
The Tasty, Economical Cookbook (Vols. 1, 2)
Sheikh and Disciple
Maya Veeram or The Forces of Illusion
Asmā'ul Husnā: The 99 Beautiful Names of Allah
Islam and World Peace: Explanations of a Sufi
A Mystical Journey
Questions of Life—Answers of Wisdom (Vols. 1, 2)
Treasures of the Heart: Sufi Stories for Young Children
To Die Before Death: The Sufi Way of Life
A Song of Muhammad ☉
Hajj: The Inner Pilgrimage
The Triple Flame: The Inner Secrets of Sufism
The Resonance of Allāh

Booklets

Gems of Wisdom series:
 Vol. 1: The Value of Good Qualities
 Vol. 2: Beyond Mind and Desire
 Vol. 3: The Innermost Heart
 Vol. 4: Come to Prayer

Pamphlets

A Contemporary Sufi Speaks:
 To Teenagers and Parents
 On the Signs of Destruction
 On Peace of Mind
 On the True Meaning of Sufism
 On Unity: The Legacy of the Prophets
 The Meaning of Fellowship
 Mind, Desire, and the Billboards of the World

Foreign Language Publications
 Ein Zeitgenössischer Sufi Spricht über Inneren Frieden
 (A Contemporary Sufi Speaks on Peace of Mind—
 German translation)

 Deux Discours tirés du Livre L'Islam et la Paix Mondiale:
 Explications d'un Soufi
 (Two Discourses from the Book, Islam and World Peace:
 Explanations of a Sufi—French translation)

For free catalog or book information call:
(888) 786-1786
or fax: (215) 879-6307
Web Address: http://www.bmf.org

About
The Bawa Muhaiyaddeen Fellowship

Muhammad Raheem Bawa Muhaiyaddeen ☺, a Sufi mystic from Sri Lanka, was a man of extraordinary wisdom and compassion. For over seventy years he shared his knowledge and experience with people of every race and religion and from all walks of life.

The central branch of The Bawa Muhaiyaddeen Fellowship is in Philadelphia, Pennsylvania, which was M. R. Bawa Muhaiyaddeen's home when he lived in the United States before his death in December, 1986. The Fellowship continues to serve as a meeting house, and as a reservoir of people and materials for everyone who is interested in his teachings.

The Mosque of Shaikh Muhammad Raheem Bawa Muhaiyaddeen is located on the same property; here the five daily prayers and Friday congregational prayers are observed. An hour west of the Fellowship is the *Mazār*, the tomb of M. R. Bawa Muhaiyaddeen ☺ which is open daily between sunrise and sunset.

For further information write or phone:

The Bawa Muhaiyaddeen Fellowship
5820 Overbrook Avenue
Philadelphia, Pennsylvania 19131

(215) 879-6300

E-mail Address: info@bmf.org
Web Address: http://www.bmf.org

If you would like to visit the Fellowship, or to obtain a schedule of current events, branch locations and meetings, please write, phone or E-mail *Attn: Visitor Information.*

Made in the USA